Charlotte Ward is a print j e
writer. *It's Not Me, It's Yo* es
with her beau in London.

By Charlotte Ward

Why Am I Always the One Before 'The One'?

It's Not Me, It's You

CHARLOTTE WARD

headline

First published in 2009
by HEADLINE PUBLISHING GROUP

1

Cataloguing in Publication Data is available from the British Library

978 0 7553 1887 2

Typeset in Sabon by Avon DataSet Ltd,
Bidford-on-Avon, Warwickshire

Printed and bound in Great Britain by
Clays Ltd, St Ives plc

Headline's policy is to use papers that are natural, renewable and
recyclable products and made from wood grown in sustainable forests. The
logging and manufacturing processes are expected to conform to the
environmental regulations of the country of origin.

HEADLINE PUBLISHING GROUP
An Hachette UK Company
338 Euston Road
London NW1 3BH

www.headline.co.uk
www.hachette.co.uk
www.charlotteward.net

For Mum and Fitzsy,
thank you for everything.

Introduction

I'll never forget the first time I was dumped. I was ten years old and the yellow-bellied swine didn't even do it himself. Chris Wallace was my best friend Clare's gorgeous older brother. He had nice freckles, a touch of the ginge (hot!) and skinny little legs. I thought he was just heavenly.

Our ill-fated love affair began in the summer holidays when I'd frequently cycle round to the Wallace household to hang out with Clare (and secretly gaze at Chris). We'd pass the time climbing trees, experimenting with Clare's mum's make-up and singing along to 'I Should Be So Lucky'. Chris didn't like Kylie much. He preferred Michael Jackson. That didn't matter to me. He was cool and I was smitten.

When our childish romance began it wasn't as if we kissed or anything – yuck, we were far too young for that – but, at some point, Chris definitely asked me to be his girlfriend and I was over-the-moon.

Chris, being a boy about town, had had girlfriends before, but he was my very first boyfriend. It was all new and exciting to me. Did we even hold hands? I don't think so, but it was the first time I can recall feeling that now oh-so-familiar feeling of butterflies in my tummy.

I'm not sure how long it lasted – maybe a couple of

weeks of exchanging toothy grins and trading stickers for *Neighbours* albums. I couldn't have been happier, but on our first day back at school after the summer, tragedy struck. During the lunch break, I was sitting on the playing fields with my friends making daisy chains, when two cool girls from my year approached. They didn't beat about the bush.

'Chris sent us,' they told me menacingly, like two mini Mitchell brothers on *EastEnders*. 'He says you're not his girlfriend any more.'

As they walked off, I sat there forlornly pulling out daisy petals one by one and chanting miserably under my breath, 'He loves me, he loves me not . . .' I think I sulked through my lessons for the rest of the day. Later, I was horrified to discover that the word on the playground was that Chris was now 'going out' with Lindsay – one of the girls he'd dispatched to break the bad news. Simply charming.

But, although I contemplated stabbing Lindsay (or Chris) with my maths compass, it was an important rite of passage for me. It was the very first time I got to experience the old heave-ho, and firmly set the wheels in motion for many years of heartache, despair and humiliation. And don't even get me started on the moaning, obsessing, paranoia, self-loathing, hatred of all men, begging, crying, self-centred monopolisation of conversations, general nuttiness and bunny boiler moments.

And yet, as I circumnavigated my single years, there was also euphoria, excitement, wild nights out and comical (still slightly drunk) post-mortem phone calls to friends the following morning, the intrigue of flirting with a handsome chap while your coupled-up friend enviously sits there knowing she has to behave, and the empowerment of realising it's perfectly fine not to rely on a man. And, yes, life does go on.

You see, whoever said breaking up was hard to do (every blinking time) was clearly far too busy crying into their Chardonnay. Yes, sometimes splitting up can be brutal. It can come when you least expect it and when you have no choice in the matter.

However it happens, it hurts like hell and, to add insult to injury, there is often a ridiculous amount of crap to deal with afterwards. As well as coping with the small things (which seem colossal when you are gripped by grief), like dividing CDs, shoving your photo frames face down in the drawer, and trying to form sentences without your voice wobbling, you may be forced to get to grips with even weightier issues, like moving out before your lease is up, still working with him every day, or the fact that he has just seduced your best friend. Sometimes, you just can't avoid the initial acrid odour of break-ups – it stinks.

But – and it's a big but – hand-on-heart, how many of us have actually ended up like Miss Havisham from *Great Expectations*? OK, you may have just been dumped, but are you presently lying bereft on the hearth all wrinkled and bitter, wearing a shabby wedding dress and awaiting that final spark from the fire to fast-track you in a fireball to meet your maker? Nope. A bit battered, a bit bruised maybe, but not attempting a hearth-arsed death like Miss H. (Quite right too, she's a work of fiction and it wasn't a happy ending.)

Now, without meaning to be insensitive, aren't most break-ups actually quite easy once you get past those first few painful weeks of self-pity and wallowing? Isn't it occasionally *you* that tells that no-good, dead-weight rotter exactly where he can stick his relationship?

And if, God forbid, he did the ditching, how amazing is it when finally the worm turns and you can embrace life without him once more? There's that moment of divine inspiration as you pound the pavement jubilantly, listening to 'Survivor' by Destiny's Child on your iPod. (I'm not ashamed to admit I've done this and I promise you that caterwauling along to that song is like therapy – incidentally, we'll be covering empowering songs later.)

The thing is, being as po-faced as Posh is actually quite exhausting after a while. You've got to see the light eventually and life has a funny way of presenting you with humour – even during your darkest hours of misery.

Isn't it really quite amusing when, in the perfect act of divine retribution, the ex who claimed he was too busy for a relationship is made redundant, or simply realises the error of his ways and begs you to take him back, to no avail? Who could help but snigger when friends kindly point out that the new bird he's been tagged with on Facebook is actually a complete troll?

Just because your relationship is dead to the world doesn't mean you are – in contrast, now is the perfect time to pull all the fit, single men for whom you've always felt a simmering, underlying sexual tension. And what about the fact that you get to experience a heady kind of hot boy pick-and-mix now that you're back out in single society?

If you're feeling miserable about a man, if you're heart is broken, this book is your first step to rehabilitation. It's time for an adult, angsty, show-and-tell extravaganza, with more break-up stories than you can shake a stick at. So stop sleeping with that smelly old sweater of his, tear up that stack of old anniversary and Valentine's cards, and dig out those pulling pants.

Over the course of these pages you'll find real-life stories of pain, pathos and self-pity from women (and men), told with dark humour, that will help you see that things aren't really all that bad.

You'll also discover plenty of cheeky and inspiring tales from footloose and fancy-free fillies who fully embrace singledom. In fact, whether you're the owner of a broken heart or a blissfully happy one, a devoted singleton or happily married with children, you're likely to enjoy many of the weepy, wicked and wanton stories. It's an exciting world out there – so read on and be prepared for some intense laughter therapy . . .

1.

First love, first snub

Occasionally I've met (in different incarnations) a smug girl who will smile and remark, 'You know, I've never been dumped . . .'

In an ideal world it would be great if the rest of us could totter around feeling nice and superior too. But what Miss Smug hasn't caught on to yet is that being dumped is a crucial learning curve.

In a way, it's like backing up your computer hard drive. When everything crashes and corrupts, you know that somewhere in the ether you have the vital information to reboot and rebuild. In contrast, when the message finally reads 'abort, retry, fail' for Miss Smug, without back-up or any experience of a break-up she'll have to start right back at the beginning.

As my friend Georgina wisely points out: 'You've got to learn the hard way to turn a negative into a positive. If I hadn't been dumped from such a great height by such lowly men I wouldn't now be living it up with such a great guy.'

And, no doubt, without those excruciating break-up stories that leave our friends gasping with shock and awe, life would be very dull indeed.

One of the most memorable ways I was shown the red card was when I witnessed the chap I was seeing at the time snogging not one but *four* other girls in our local nightclub.

I first met Jake at college. He was tall with dark hair and one of those wedge haircuts (curtains on top and shaved underneath – dead trendy back in 1995, hideous now, obviously.) As far as I was concerned, Jake was a dreamboat. If he even looked in my direction, I'd be close to hyperventilating.

We'd hang out in the dirty, smelly smoker's room of the college canteen, sitting at grubby plastic tables. I didn't even smoke but would happily sit in there trying not to choke on the rancid fumes just to get a little bit of his attention. I thought it was the start of something new and exciting.

After weeks of flirting, I finally managed to pull Jake at Golddiggers, a rather rubbish nightclub in Wiltshire, which all the under-age kids seemed to frequent. Golddiggers was not a classy venue. The music sounded distorted and the carpets were sticky. Every Friday and Saturday night it was packed full of clearly under-age sixteen- and seventeen-year-olds getting plastered on horrible alcopops like Hooch and Woody's. In fact, one week I downed so many revolting sickly sweet day-glow drinks (probably only about three) that I actually kept falling over on the dance floor – much to my friends' amusement.

Anyway, after Jake had wowed me on the dance floor with his magnificent moves, we finally puckered up under the straining sounds of 'Cotton Eye Joe' by Rednex or some equally appalling nineties tune.

I cannot tell you how swoony I was. For the next few weeks, Jake consumed my every waking thought. At college

I checked my make-up and hair about a zillion times a day and lost count of the number of times I headed into the canteen under the pretence of picking up another can of Fanta or a Twirl chocolate bar. When I did see Jake, he kept me weak at the knees by acting cool but interested, and I was thrilled to be invited to hang out at his house a couple of times (for more snogging) after college.

Well that was that, I was hooked. It didn't even put me off when his younger brother slyly revealed that Jake regularly practised his dancing in front of the mirror in his bedroom. But just as I started to imagine sweetly that we would be together for ever, I got a short sharp shock.

That Friday night I'd taken a great deal of trouble to get ready. I was wearing knee-high boots, a silver metallic miniskirt and a lilac pink T-shirt, emblazoned with 'Handle With Care' across my chest (I was a very sophisticated young lady in those days). I'd also plaited little sections of my hair on either side as I'd seen Angel, Melissa George's character on *Home and Away*, do.

When I arrived at 'Diggers', as it was nicknamed, I discovered from one of Jake's friends that he was indeed in the vicinity, but it was quite some time (and several drinks later) before I actually spied him. As I walked into the foyer area of the club where quite a crowd were hanging out, I suddenly froze as I spied Jake with a girl in a corner of the room. His head was angled towards hers and, to my horror, he began kissing her. As I stood there, tears beginning to fall, it seemed to last a lifetime. Jake's eyes were closed and his fingers were entwined in her hair. Like a car-crash scene, I couldn't stop rubbernecking.

Finally, they came up for air and the girl wandered off. Overcome by rage, I seized my chance and stormed over to Jake. He was now talking to his friend and laughing. He didn't see me coming until the last minute and by then it was too late. My hand was raised and, taking a clear swing, I slapped him hard across the cheek. As he stared at me, his face full of shock and disdain, I turned on my heels and ran off sobbing to find my friends. For the rest of the night I wept, drowned my sorrows with Archers and lemonade, and watched with increasing dismay as an angry Jake prowled around the nightclub kissing various other girls (I counted three more).

Eventually, another young chap saw that one man's trash was another man's treasure and decided to chat me up. This despite the fact I looked like a red-eyed hag. Although the attention temporarily numbed my pain, I was gutted about Jake and dreaded seeing him at college the following week. Then, surprisingly, when I did bump into him he was pretty gracious.

'I had that slap mark on my face for three days!' he told me. 'But my mum said I deserved it. The thing is, Charlotte, I'm not cut out for relationships. I think I'll be an eternal bachelor.'

Well, that gave me some comfort – it wasn't me, it was him.

But then, a week later, I heard that Jake was going out with Jayne, one of the girls he'd snogged on the same night that I'd slapped him. He ended up going out with her for TWO YEARS.

It was me.

The wonder years

So let's start right at the beginning, shall we?

Who could forget the losing their virginity scenes in the film *American Pie*? There's the relationship between lovebirds Oz and Heather, which results in a very loving and romantic encounter beside a beautiful lake. Then there's Jim, who, like a rabbit in the headlights, is thrown around the room by the band geek and unlikely dominatrix Michelle. Finally, there's Finch, who, in the ultimate Mrs Robinson fantasy, is seduced by Stifler's mom on a billiards table.

An assortment of cherry-popping opportunities – just like real life. Indeed, the varying experiences of losing our virginity should tell us that love and romance doesn't always go to plan.

Some lucky individuals will be able to look back on their first time with fond memories, knowing that it could be compared to Oz and Heather, within a steady relationship, involving love and tenderness, perhaps rose petals and all the other trappings of romance. In reality, there are plenty of less-than-perfect losing your virginity stories too (and which are arguably a lot more fun to share).

In my case, the whole sorry experience was blighted for many reasons, not least a rather embarrassing wardrobe malfunction. When the day arrived, I was determined to make the most of my less-than-ample teenage charms and had cunningly squeezed into a new Wonderbra. Unfortunately, it was so tight under my boobs that it dug into me like cheese wire. To solve this problem, I placed a few cotton wool pads beneath the underwiring to make it more comfortable.

I'd meant to remove them before my boyfriend, The Undeserving One, got his hands on me, but in all the build-up I'd completely forgotten. That is until, with one fell swoop, he expertly removed my bra and half a dozen bits of mangled cotton wool fell out on to the bed to remind me. Panicked, I tried to brush them to one side hoping he hadn't noticed.

Prior to this, I sat waiting nervously until The Undeserving One burst in the door clutching a bunch of wilting daisies. The gesture was slightly ruined by the fact I knew he'd grabbed them from the petrol station where his house-mate worked. But I told myself it was the thought that counts.

Upstairs, The Undeserving One put on an album of cheesy love songs and the experience just about lasted through the strains of 'True Colors' by Cindi Lauper and the aptly named 'Nothing's Gonna Stop Us Now' by Starship. Afterwards, I suddenly felt overwhelmed and insecure. The enormity of what I'd done hit me, and I felt very emotional and started crying.

Although at the time The Undeserving One did his best to comfort me, I was devastated to learn that the following day he'd held court in the pub about our intimate encounter. 'She cried and her bra was stuffed with cotton wool!' he'd announced to hoots of laughter from his friends.

And, not only did he kiss and tell, he also cracked the same rubbish joke to anyone who'd listen, saying, 'Do you remember your eighteenth? I do, her name was Charlotte!'

Now you know why he's called The Undeserving One.

Recalling that story still makes my skin crawl. Occasionally, like some kind of psycho, I'll Google The Undeserving One and feel sick when I find pictures of him. I can't believe it still sparks such an extreme reaction in me, but there's no denying that so often it is our first love that seems to have the biggest impact on us.

When you are young and have just fallen head-over-heels for the very first time, it's perfectly normally to rush forward with wild abandon. With no previous heartache to prompt warning signs in your head, you go for it, hell for leather, assuming that everything will be fine and dandy.

If it ends abruptly, then, quite frankly, you are stuffed.

There could not have been a more hideous fate for sweet and innocent Harriet than being targeted by a self-styled 'virgin-hunter' named Marcus.

The cruel hand of fate conspired for Harriet, a girl who had managed to keep her virginity intact until the impressive age of twenty-three, to meet Marcus at a party. Sadly, she got drunk, got charmed and was humped and dumped, all expertly manoeuvred within a twelve-hour window of the virgin-hunter's heavy schedule.

Harriet had no idea what to expect and after five minutes of foreplay, she spent the majority of the experience struggling to switch the light off as Marcus confidently turned it back on. The next morning he took her to the station and that was the last she heard of him. Thus began a lifetime of regret.

But if we could offer a small, but none the less positive take on poor Harriet's humiliation, it would be that the dastardly act took place in a bed.

Sometimes, not only is the whole experience traumatic, but the setting sucks too . . .

In the summer before heading off to university, Jennifer decided that her virginal days were numbered.

'I was stupidly convinced that I just had to do the deed,' she reveals. 'So I told my rather gleeful boyfriend that I wanted to lose it during a camping trip that we had planned.

'On the first day we went for a tough hike and became lost. It was dark and we were both cranky. By the time we got down to it, the heavens had opened and the tent was leaking. It couldn't have been less romantic or technically awkward. Every so often, my boyfriend would be forced to stop and pour water out of my boots, which were filling with rain water.'

Afterwards, Jennifer had envisaged the two of them lying together, romantically stroking each other's hair and gazing at each other lovingly. In reality, they huddled together shivering in a dripping tent, clutching damp sleeping bags and trying to ward off hypothermia.

Jennifer adds: 'Occasionally, during the night I'd wake with a yelp as my boyfriend accidentally whacked me as he attempted to punch water up and out of the straining, rain-soaked sides of the tent. It was one of the worst nights of my life.'

In another traumatic tent experience, Polly recalls 'losing it' in the summer of 1988.

'I was fifteen and living in a hot country, so I spent most of my time wearing a bikini the size of a teabag and not much else,' she reveals. 'He was eighteen and utterly gorgeous. I spotted him at a beach party and, after getting thoroughly fuelled up on vodka and orange, was dared by my mates to chat him up. This I did, and fast forward several hours and many more vodkas, I somehow found myself back in his tent, minus bikini.

'My abiding memory of the "all-important moment" when I crossed the bridge from girl to woman was hearing Yazz's "The Only Way Is Up" playing from the nearby beach party.' How very apt.

'I threw up on him shortly afterwards, and started crying when I realised that we had been the floor show, as several of his mates had been ogling the whole event through the tent flaps.

'To this day, I cannot hear Yazz without experiencing a brief moment of utter humiliation, and thanking the Lord that mobile phones and YouTube had not been invented.'

Our next foray into the work of womanhood comes courtesy of a candid young lady called Danielle, who admits that not only did she lose her virginity in the back of a car, but afterwards had immense trouble even recalling who the lucky man was.

'I was a very naive seventeen year old and at the time had the "hots" for two friends called Brian and Tom.

Confusingly, I had fallen for the lovely gentlemanly reputation of Tom, but the looks of ladykiller Brian.

'So, consequently, I was very excited to see them both at a friend's rave party on a balmy summer's evening – so excited that I got very merry and needed a little lie down.'

Drunk and sleepy Danielle curled up on a blanket by a big bonfire in the garden. It was then that tragedy almost struck.

'In my drunken haze, it was all terribly cosy.' she says, 'I managed to fall asleep completely oblivious of the dangers – and was soon precariously rolling towards the fire.

'Next thing I knew, I was woken by my knight in shining armour, one of my crushes – either Tom or Brian – although as I had slight double vision I couldn't quite decide.

'After my hero had saved me, we went for a little walk, or should I say sway, so that I could sober up. It was then that Brian/Tom asked if I would like to see his car. Although I was somewhat deflated to see a battered Ford Fiesta parked in the lane, I sat inside to listen to the new Leftfield album with him.'

Somewhere around track three, Danielle's suddenly less than gentlemanly suitor ushered her into the back seat of his cramped car for 'a bit of a cuddle'.

'It was all a bit of an anticlimax,' she relates, 'although the next day I was convinced I'd lost it to lovely Tom. Sadly, it transpired that – surprise, surprise – I'd actually done the deed with Brian the womaniser. Either way, I didn't land a boyfriend and it was not AT ALL how I pictured it all happening.'

* * *

In yet another tale of anguish, Hayley reveals she was the talk of the playground, for all the wrong reasons.

'When I was fourteen (yes, fourteen), I was desperately in love with a boy from the year above,' she says. 'Although we were friends, he didn't really pay me much attention. Anyway, roll on the school Christmas disco, when he and five mates turned up absolutely hammered. I bumped into him in the cloakroom and I was pleasantly surprised to notice that he was drunkenly flirting with me.'

Although the object of her affection was promptly thrown out of the disco for being under the influence, a smitten Hayley followed.

'We ended up snogging in the playground and then actually having sex standing up against the wall of the school hall,' she admits red-faced. 'It was over in minutes and the next day I made the mistake of telling my so-called best friend, who managed to spread it around the whole school within a couple of hours.

'Even worse, he denied everything because he couldn't remember a thing. This meant that half the school considered me a slapper for doing it, whilst the other half thought I was a slapper for making it up!

'He still claims amnesia to this day, but a few years ago when I bumped into him he finally relented, saying, "Oh well, if you still say it happened then I suppose it must have!"'

In hindsight, perhaps my own cotton wool calamity wasn't quite so bad . . .

But whether your tricky first venture into the world of

amour resulted in just five minutes of drunken fumbling (or, if you were really lucky, something more substantial), it seems the worst thing any of us could do is allow a painful first love experience to become the benchmark for all future relationships. Most agree there is no worse feeling than having your heart trampled on for the very first time. It's like a bomb going off – total carnage with the possibility of life-long scars thrown in.

But did you know that scientists recently discovered that the euphoric feelings of our first encounter of love can often give us unrealistic ideals about future romances? According to a report from a British university, those who strive to relive the intense passion of their first love often end up disappointed.

Admittedly, puppy love can be a bit ridiculous. When you fall for the first time, all practicalities go out the window. It's just about him and you and being together at all costs. And if, as so often is the case, your parents don't approve or would rather you knuckled down to your GCSEs, that's even more incentive to view yourselves as a modern-day Romeo and Juliet.

But at some point you have to grow up. Our first loves might have had a massive effect on us, whether good or bad, but eventually you have to move on (so says the girl who still feverishly Googles hers – oops).

One of the more humbling experiences on the trail of love is when you realise that your would-be suitor does not share the same view from your rose-tinted specs.

Being the one who apparently misread the signals as to how well the relationship was going is painfully humiliating.

Sometimes we believe we are right in the midst of love's young dream before we realise that the other person's agenda is concealed . . .

Kerry was nineteen when she fell head-over-heels for her first love Simon, a twenty-four-year-old tour manager.

'The minute I set eyes on him it was all about getting that man,' she recalls. 'He had these lovely brown puppy dog eyes, was cocky, funny and confident, and I loved him instantly.'

At the time, Kerry was a backing singer with the group Simon was managing, and he'd just broken up with his girlfriend.

'We started seeing each other during the tour and slept together within two weeks,' she says. 'Sometimes he'd talk about his ex-girlfriend, Liz, but seeing as she was thirty, which in my nineteen-year-old mind was "really old", I didn't see her as a threat.'

Indeed, Kerry even took it in her stride when Liz turned up at a New Year's Eve party. 'We were introduced and she seemed nice enough,' she recalls. 'I even remember her telling me in her thick Brummie accent, "Go for it with Simon, he really likes ya."'

When the tour came to an end, Kerry and Simon continued to see each other when they could. 'It was hard, as I was on tour with another band and he was back at his flat in London, but we'd try and get together about once a week,' she says. 'It was in the days before mobile phones so I would call his landline from phone boxes whenever I could.

'Occasionally, he wouldn't be able to meet me but I might come back to wherever my digs were to find a love letter. It felt like raw, passionate love and I was besotted.'

To Kerry's delight, it wasn't long before Simon asked her to live with him. 'I was thrilled and started to make plans to move into his flat as soon as I was back from the tour,' she adds. 'But not long after, I started to suspect he was going cold on me. The more needy I got, the more stand-offish he seemed.

'My tour finished in Bristol and on the last day I called Simon's home number. When the phone was answered by a girl with a Brummie accent, I immediately hung up.

'Then, standing trembling in the phone box, I fumbled in my pockets for more change and called back. "It's Kerry here," I said when the girl answered again. "Can I ask you a question?"

' "Hold on a minute while I turn the telly down," she replied.

'I then stood there shaking for what seemed like a year until she came back on the line. "I'm not being funny," I told her. "But I'm supposed to be moving in with Simon in a week's time and I'm just confused as to why you are there?"

'It was then that she paused. "Oh dear. Hasn't he told ya?" she replied.

It turned out she was the one Simon wanted – and she was the one who was moving all her stuff in.

'At that moment it felt as though my heart had snapped in two. I couldn't breathe. It was like being punched very hard in the stomach. I loved the bones off him; I loved the smell of him. I actually thought I'd have his kids.

'About an hour later, I had to perform on stage with the band and I spent the whole set singing with tears streaming down my cheeks. That night I called up my friend, she scooped me up and took me back to her mum's house, where I slept in the spare room in a little single bed and cried myself to sleep.

'It was a very bleak time. Simon didn't even call me afterwards. I spent days calling and calling, and when I finally reached him, he was really off with me. "I thought you'd get it," he said. "It's not happening."

'At that moment, something just shut down in me. I've never had my heart broken like that since.'

But no matter how much it hurt at the time, Kerry admits she got over it. Just like we all do.

Of course, Kerry was not the first or the last young lady to have been given the supposed green light in a relationship, only to have the rug pulled from under her feet at a later date.

Cheryl, now happily married, revealed how she was so besotted with her first love that she nearly sabotaged every relationship that followed. She first met Pete, the object of her undying affection, when she was just thirteen years old. Two years older and the cousin of her best friend Katie, Pete lived and went to school thirty miles away from Cheryl's hometown.

'I just fell for him instantly. It really was love at first sight,' she says, 'and I think he felt exactly the same. We first kissed not long after my fourteenth birthday and from that moment I was hooked!'

Over the next few years Cheryl and Pete met up whenever he was visiting his family. But at that age the distance hindered them and the relationship seemed impossible. By the time Cheryl turned sixteen, she found herself going out with Richie, a local boy from school.

'He was the nicest person you could ever meet, but he didn't stand a chance when Pete was around,' Cheryl admits. 'That summer Katie and I had bought tickets for the Reading Festival, and when she called to say that Pete also had a ticket, I just went potty. All I could think about was spending three whole days with Pete, and so I immediately called up Richie and unceremoniously dumped him. He was heartbroken, but all I could think about was Pete.'

The night before the festival Cheryl received a call from Richie to ask if he could travel to Reading with her and Katie as he was meeting friends there. The last thing Cheryl wanted was her ex tagging along, but she didn't have the heart to say no and just assumed he'd do his own thing.

But when they arrived at the campsite, it was clear Richie was in no hurry to meet his pals and, embarrassingly, he watched as she greeted Pete with squeals of delight.

'I was totally obsessed,' Cheryl admits. 'So when we all decided to go to a club in town, all I wanted was to have Pete to myself.'

Although at first Cheryl kept her flirty behaviour in check, after a few drinks she no longer cared whether Richie was there to see or not.

'I spent the night glued to Pete's side,' she confesses. 'Richie witnessed it all, including us kissing. He looked really hurt but didn't say a word.'

Late at night they traipsed back to the campsite in the rain to discover Cheryl and Katie's tent had flooded. Conveniently, the girls had no choice but to sleep in Pete's tent. It was at this point that Richie threw a spanner in the works. He hadn't bought a tent, had no friends at the festival and the whole thing was just a ploy to try and win Cheryl back.

'I was hopping mad. He was ruining my chances with Pete. I told him huffily that he could sleep in the tent porch and brazenly snuggled into Pete's sleeping bag.'

That night, loosened up by alcohol, Cheryl and Pete did a lot more than just kiss, as all the while a shivering Richie lay heartbroken barely half a metre away.

But the next day it was Cheryl who was left distraught. In the sober light of day, Pete didn't want to know. Devastated and sick from too much cider, she broke down and found comfort from an unlikely source – reliable Richie. 'I was such a bitch but after everything I'd done to him, it was Richie who looked after me,' she reveals.

'I saw Pete a few more times during the next year, but one day I received a bombshell. Katie informed me that Pete was going to be a dad: he'd had a one-night-stand at university and the girl was pregnant. They had decided to make a go of it and planned to have the baby. I was absolutely gutted.

'He was my one true love but now everything was ruined. I knew then that we'd never be together, but for almost the next decade I irrationally viewed him as "the one who got away".

'After that, I wrecked nearly every subsequent

relationship, thinking that nobody could ever compare. It was really only when I met my future husband that I realised I had to allow myself to move on. I suddenly saw that over the years I'd been using my early memories as a defence mechanism to stop myself from falling for people. In short, I'd sabotaged my own love life.

'Now that I've allowed myself to fall completely head-over-heels with someone else, it's great. I love being married and have finally laid the ghosts of what could have been to rest.'

Of course, sometimes you look back at your first love with utter mortification at how cheesy the whole thing was . . .

'My first love was a German guy called Otto,' says Rosemary. 'He was blond, six feet four and gorgeous. We'd get stoned together, snog, and stare into each other's eyes whilst he'd murmur what I thought were enchanting sweet somethings. The warning signs should have been the walls of self-portraits that adorned his bedroom and the flowery one-liners. He said we were "the Prince and Princess who met under a star".

'Otto was, and still is, the most romantic man I had ever met – but it wasn't until I was dumped "by poem" that I realised what a narcissistic idiot he really was.

'It was only after our little fairytale had ended that I realised Otto was more the star and less the Prince in this story. I have never fallen for a man who loves himself more than me again.'

The first cut is the deepest

'I met my first love at uni and after three years, when we graduated, I wanted us to move into a flat together. He didn't seem keen so I decided to call his bluff, saying, "Well, if you don't want to move in together, we should split up." To my horror, he agreed. That'll teach me!'

'My first "proper" relationship at the age of sixteen ended with me being dumped in the most cruel, painful way. I cried for days, then screamed a bit, then cried some more. It's a bit like childbirth – when you have your first, you can't believe anything can possibly hurt that much – it's a level of pain that is wholly unimaginable. But it's never that bad again, because you're mentally prepared for it and know that there comes a point when it stops hurting and everything is fine again.'

'My first love, whom I'd been seeing for eight months, said he'd buy me a watch for my birthday, then dumped me the day before. Trouble is, it was really near Christmas, and I'd already spent a big chunk of my student loan buying him a didgeridoo. I didn't know anyone else sad enough to want one, so I marched up to his house, knocked on the door, shoved it in his hands and marched off again. The swine!'

'In my case, I developed a shell, determined that no one would ever treat me badly again. I opted for years of meaningless flings on the basis that they would be pain-free, and refused to let anyone get close. It made me fiercely independent and emotionally self-sufficient. But I wasted years thinking every man was a total shit bag and I was better off just using them before they could use me. On the upside, when I finally let my guard down and fell in love, it felt truly, properly right.'

'I'm still crazy about my first love after eighteen years. I saw him the other day. He's high-flying but still single, still totally fucked up and – guess what – so am I now!'

Not long after The Undeserving One took my virginity, he trashed my heart as well. Indeed, it was an obsession with *his* first love that added to a long list of reasons the relationship was doomed to fail.

The night he chose to dump me was his housemate's twenty-first birthday party. Among the guests was a very pretty girl called Victoria, with beautiful shiny, waist-length hair. It transpired The Undeserving One had gone out with this lovely lady a couple of years earlier. He'd kindly pointed her out and explained that in his mind her parents had split them up.

To my dismay, throughout the evening, he seemed to

grow more and more obsessed with her. He basically ignored me, his eyes following her round the party, while I drank myself into oblivion.

At the end of the night, once all the guests had gone, I found The Undeserving One sitting on the floor. He had his head down and was holding a birthday card. He looked sad, and when I knelt down next to him, I saw that the card he was gazing at was from Victoria and he was tracing his fingers over her handwriting.

'Oh, for God's sake, just get over it,' I snapped at him. 'Her parents split you up? Do me a favour! I'm sure if she'd really wanted to be with you she would have found a way!'

The Undeserving One immediately spun round, his face twisted with anger, and a massive row ensued. Eventually, he told me he didn't want to go out with me any more. As I sobbed, he demanded I leave there and then, as he had work the next day and I'd 'stop him from sleeping'.

It was very late and I lived miles away with my parents, so I made a distraught phone call to my friend Andrew and arranged to stay with him. When I arrived, he kindly fed me tea and biscuits and sat up with me while I sobbed into the wee small hours.

To be honest, the next few weeks were pretty horrible. I headed home to my parents and stomped around the house being moody and snapping at everyone for no reason at all.

One day, my older cousins took me out and got me drunk in a bid to cheer me up. But the alcohol only fuelled my anguish, so I headed home and immediately drunk-dialled The Undeserving One. After just a few minutes of my inebriated ramblings, he hung up on me. I then had a big fight with my mother, my father shouted at me and, like a true drama queen, I crumpled on to the sofa, sobbing and wailing loudly.

I think Dad told me to pull myself together but Mum was more patient. 'Leave her,' I overheard her saying. 'She's had her heart broken for the first time.'

It must have been just as heartbreaking for her to see me in such a state, acting like the world was over. I honestly dread the day I have children of my own and have to see them go through it for the first time. It was bad enough seeing it happen to my little sister! I wonder how many parents flick through the *Yellow Pages* longing for a section entitled 'hit men' or, at the very best, 'leg breaking'?

But, as the benefit of hindsight proves, the pain doesn't last for ever. I think the turning point for me came on New Year's Eve that year, a good few weeks after The Undeserving One had given me the official heave-ho. I went to a nightclub in Bristol with a couple of friends, and at midnight found a fairly decent chap to pucker up with. He told me his name was Dave, and later, as we sat in a booth chatting, he revealed that he too had recently been callously dumped.

'I just feel so rejected,' he told me.

'I know! Me too,' I agreed.

'She was so cruel,' he sighed.

'Yeah, he was so mean,' I nodded.

We spent the next few hours indulging in a kind of sad bastard heartbreak one-upmanship. Then, at the end of the night, we dutifully swapped numbers, knowing full well that we had no intention of calling each other.

When I looked at his piece of paper I saw he'd scribbled the name Paul. 'I thought you said your name was Dave?' I asked.

'Sorry, I made that up,' he admitted. 'Paul is quite a boring name so I decided to pretend to be someone else.'

Rather cruelly, I began to understand why his girlfriend had dumped him. It was also a breakthrough moment that made me realise I wasn't going to sit around any more and wallow.

The next day, I woke up feeling enlightened. It was time to forget about The Undeserving One and get on with my life. I wasn't remotely interested in Dave or Paul or whatever the hell his name was, but just discovering that I was mildly attractive to someone else and had actually enjoyed kissing him was enough to set me off on the road to recovery.

Likewise, being able to speak to someone who had also been through the mill made me realise that 'shit happens' and life goes on.

Of course, not everyone has a brutal first love experience to get over. Some lucky souls have the kind of nauseating stories that could inspire a sickly Jennifer Lopez romance film, and I suppose we should begrudgingly acknowledge that.

Ella is one of them . . .

'My first love was at the age of thirteen. I had recently left an all-girls' boarding school so was like a parched traveller crawling out of the desert into an oasis of teenage boys,' she reveals. 'I first saw him air-guitaring to Dire Straits at a party, after which he tipped lemonade on my head and asked me to get off with him (for this is what one did in 1986). It was my first proper kiss and I was utterly smitten – we went out together for six months until I left the country for four years, an occasion he marked by giving me Nick Kamen's 'Each Time You Break My Heart' on seven-inch vinyl. I thought I would die of grief every time I played it.

'Our lives went off in very different directions but we have always kept in touch. Twenty-three years later, we have ended up living in neighbouring villages and he is my son's godfather. Now isn't that a nice story?'

It is a nice story – and it makes you realise that it's often too easy, when looking back at break-ups, to recount only the stories where you were the victim. If the truth be known, the majority of us have not only been on the receiving end of some fairly discourteous behaviour but we've dished it out too.

Just like Jess, who had been dating Callum for just a couple of months, when she figured she was not really that into him.

'Callum was getting really serious very quickly,' she says. 'A couple of months in he'd declared his love for me but I wasn't ready to say it back. We were just getting to know each other.'

Poor smitten Callum kept trying to work out how Jess really felt about him and rather sneakily saw the fact that she mumbled in her sleep as an opportunity to find out.

'One night I had been sleep talking a bit, but when

Callum started asking questions, I was actually awake, so I decided to play along. When he asked if I loved him, I decided that now was as good a time as any to say no.'

With his affections rebuffed, Callum grew ever more fretful that he would lose Jess and, when he found out she was still in touch with her ex, he panicked. 'Suddenly he became obsessed with the idea that we should move to Canada,' she says. 'He started researching jobs on the Internet and sending me links. I just thought he was insane.'

Meanwhile, Callum's twenty-fifth birthday was approaching and, in a last ditch attempt to give the relationship a chance, Jess booked a posh restaurant and hotel.

'On his birthday we went for dinner and Callum just kept gazing at me the whole time and saying, "I love you so much." In fact, he was so busy smiling soppily at me, that his food fell off his fork and into the gravy on his plate, splattering his shirt. I just couldn't hide the look of disgust on my face.

' "What?" he asked. So I told him I didn't want to go out with him any more. We finished dinner in silence with Callum looking as though he would dissolve into tears at any moment.'

Jess openly admits it wasn't her finest moment, and that she got her come-uppance not long after. 'The guy I dated after Callum I messed around a bit too. Ian was really into me but, just as with his predecessor, his keenness panicked me. After a year I suddenly broke it off.'

Ian was stunned and very upset. But after a couple of weeks, Jess had a change of heart. She told Ian she'd made a mistake and they were soon back together.

'The first time we slept together, following our recon-ciliation, the condom split,' she reveals. 'I just thought, "Oh my God, I'm pregnant!" But as my aunty worked at the local family planning clinic, there was no way I was going there.

'So, after a great deal of fuss, we found another clinic where I was given the morning-after pill. Well, I was sick all night, while Ian slept soundly. The next day, I lay in bed feeling a little better and remarked, "Well, at least we're back together."

'But Ian had a weird look on his face. "The thing is," he told me, "I don't know if I love you."'

Then, as Jess lay there gawping, he walked out to have a shower. 'When he came back he just looked at me scornfully and said, "Are you still here?" He then bundled me out of the house and walked me to the bus stop. I guess I got a taste of my own medicine!'

Karma does seem to feature heavily in the relationship merry-go-round – could you take what you dish out? Equally, next time your heart is smashed by a complete rotter, just remember that sooner or later his bad behaviour might be rewarded with the perfect poetic justice.

Sally was going out with a barman who was also a musician in his spare time. He and his mates had been trying to get a contract with a label for a long time and he was obsessed by music.

Sally was happy to look after them all, fetching them food and drink and keeping the flat tidy. She looked after her man's every need, even though he was only occasionally in the mood for sex. She also held down two jobs and looked after her whole family. But the day came when she was casually cast aside.

It seems she was getting too demanding and he needed to concentrate on his career.

Sally was devastated. But over the months that followed, she started to bloom again; she went out dancing and on trips with her friends.

She began to realise that she had been holed up in a smoky flat for far too long, trying to get the attention of a man who was indifferent to whether she was there or not, unless of course he happened to feel lonely. She started to feel like a woman again, not just the domestic help.

The karma part? Well, it was completely unintentional on Sally's part, but while mixing with her old circle, she started going to more and more parties, and one night she met a guy who couldn't keep his eyes off her. They fell in love. He had time for her. He didn't find her demanding at all. And he successfully managed to balance his career with loving her.

He was also a famous musician and her ex-boyfriend's hero.

The night that Sally's ex first met him, he was agog. He couldn't find words. He looked at Sally with wonder as she smiled back serenely.

Diana admits that she was particularly cruel to her ex-boyfriend Giles but only after he had finished with her, broken her heart and then decided to change his mind.

Like many men who dispatch their sweethearts, after a few months he realised that she was surviving. In fact, she was enjoying life and he didn't like it one little bit.

In a bid to woo her back, he asked her to go on a skiing holiday with him and offered to pay for everything.

'After everything he'd put me through, I was sorely tempted but said no as I didn't want to go under false pretences,' she says. 'However, he was insistent that it would be just as "good friends", so in the end I did.'

When Diana arrived in Austria, she discovered Giles had booked them into a chalet with about twenty other single people, so it was quite lively. It wasn't long before an attractive guy called James was chatting Diana up.

'Giles was particularly annoying,' she says. 'Coming on strong and completely going against his promise that he just wanted to be friends. So, I rebelled and got together with James.

'Giles then kindly informed me that I was the talk of the chalet and considered a slut. It was a small price to pay.'

The karma chronicles

'When I was in my late teens I had a really horrible boyfriend. He treated me appallingly and then broke up with me during a real low point in my life. Thankfully, I then met another guy – the complete opposite, who was lovely to me and helped me to get my self-esteem back. One day, we were walking through town laughing and joking, hand-in-hand, when I caught sight of my ex-boyfriend standing and watching me in a shop entrance. He looked utterly gutted to see me with someone else, but I felt nothing but relief that I'd left my life with him behind. It was a really uplifting moment for me.'

'He cheated on me with a girl he worked with – who then broke his heart by dumping him and going off with another work colleague. At which point he was back on my doorstep full of regret. I told him it was too little, too late.'

'One boyfriend broke up with me and then accident-ally got shot in the face by an air rifle two weeks later. He was OK but still has a scar on his cheek. He was a complete arse, so I like to think it's karma.'

'I was really making an effort with a guy I liked but he'd always cancel our dates at the last minute. After two months he broke up with me, citing that his job was just too demanding for a girlfriend. Then three weeks later, I heard that he'd just been laid off. I'm afraid I did laugh.'

Well, that's certainly something to fill you with glee when times are tough. So, thinking back to those early days of hope, humiliation, heartache or horror, it's clear that without those crash courses in passion and love, we'd all be a bit stumped.

As each fling, blossoming romance, relationship or one-night-stand unravels, we learn a little bit more about ourselves and the limits of behaviour we are prepared to put up with.

When I was younger, I put up with some appalling treatment from blokes (and probably also dished it out), but experience taught me to establish the perimeters for future romances early on.

Falling in love for the first time is a bit like being a learner driver. At first, you are a bag of nerves attempting to manoeuvre a very alien machine. But then as things begin to go smoothly and you pass your test, you think you know it all. You get cocky, speeding round country lanes with your furry dice blowing in the wind. Then, out of the blue, you have your first near miss. You learn a lesson, lose your nerve and try to be more careful in the future.

Or, even worse, it's a full-blown collision and you land yourself in a whole host of trouble. You're left reeling, questioning everything you once thought. When you feel brave enough to get back in the driving seat, you proceed with caution, trying to avoid making the same mistakes. Yet, you still pick up the odd speeding ticket along the way.

As time goes on and you fine-tune your approach, you never forget to check your blind spot, and after running out of petrol on more than one occasion, you learn that preparation is everything.

You get to know what your dream car requires or when it's time to scrap your faithful old model. You buckle up and continue on your journey, keeping your wits about you.

But, hell, enough of the dreary motoring metaphors.

Dealing with the fallout from your first love or heartbreak has laid the foundations for romance as you know it, and with each new relationship or experience, you wise up a little bit more.

Which is why, when times get tough, you know the score. Whether your relationship is dysfunctional, miserable, passionless or just plain boring, you have the strength to stare your enemy in the face and move on.

2.

Know your enemy

The guy was perfect in every way. He was handsome, funny, had a good job and seemed kind and caring. But then over dinner he licked his knife. Suddenly, I looked at him with new eyes and saw Neanderthal man. Up to that point I'd been blinkered, ignoring nagging doubts to convince myself that he was a great catch.

I had ignored whispers from my friends that he was pretty shallow or that his haircut was very *circa* 1990 or that all the gym sessions in the world didn't change the fact that when he opened his mouth, he was actually quite boring.

'I saw Sophie eating an avocado the other day,' he smirked across the table, referring to our work pal. 'It made me laugh as not many people know they're really fattening.' Then he licked his knife again.

And in that moment, a much bigger picture suddenly came into focus, and I wanted to run for the hills. It instantly turned my stomach and doubts began to creep into my mind about him. The Repulsion had set in. And once that kind of stomach-curdling loathing has taken hold, there is usually no going back.

The Repulsion

It could be the way he continually sniffs without blowing his nose or that he sometimes can't be bothered to clean his teeth. But when The Repulsion gets really bad, any kind of physical contact can make you want to heave. We should never let a doomed relationship get to this stage – but so often we do.

There is nothing worse than when you know you just don't fancy him any more. Suddenly, a month has gone by without any action in the bedroom. There's only so many times you can rebuff his pawing advances. Every time you reject him he looks like a wounded animal.

You realise with dismay that you have got to take one for the team. So, reluctantly, you gear yourself up for it. You may have to get drunk first, turn out all the lights or close your eyes and think steamy thoughts about George Clooney. But either way it's unlikely to be any less torturous than having your fingernails removed with pliers one by one.

So, yet again, you find yourself gritting your teeth, biting down hard on the pillow and wanting to snarl, 'Will you just get it over with?' Finally, as he collapses on you, all clammy and sweaty, and starts snoring, you feel a mixture of disgust and relief. It was hideous but hopefully you can drag out another three weeks before you have to go there again.

But, the fact is, you need to be brave and end it.

It was seven months into her relationship and over the Christmas period that Faria suddenly felt The Repulsion in full flow.

'All was well at Christmas but by New Year I had gone off him!' she says. 'I just didn't fancy him any more. The only thing that was different that week was that he had visitors: an old friend of his (who I used to work with so knew quite well) and his friend's Russian girlfriend.

'I live by the sea and previously Alan had wanted me to wear a flower behind my ear when we went to the beach "like an island girl" to which, on three separate occasions, I had replied, "I'm not an island girl and it would look ridiculous."

'Then, when his visitors were there, he picked a flower and presented it to the Russian lady, saying, "A pretty flower for a pretty lady" (the same line he had used on me) and asked her to wear it behind her ear. Which she did. He then took the opportunity to whisper to me in passing, "See, it doesn't look ridiculous." (It did.)'

The next thing to rattle Faria was her chap's lack of hosting skills. When one morning Alan's guests appeared for breakfast, she was astounded to see him carrying on with his cryptic crossword at the dining-room table and ignoring them.

'I was amazed by his rudeness,' Faria explains. 'I said, "Alan, your guests are ready for breakfast." And he said, "Go ahead, I've had mine." I reluctantly cooked breakfast for them, but what was I? A lackey or something?'

But the killer Repulsion moment came for Faria on New Year's Eve when Alan suggested playing a card game.

'We were all chatting when he suggested we play bridge. He had tried to teach me how to play it before but I told him I didn't enjoy it, mainly because he was overenthusiastic in his pleasure at beating me. It was my first game for heaven's sake! So when he suggested it on New Year's Eve I said no. The Russian lady said she didn't know how to play the game, so I thought he would drop it, but no, he spent half an hour explaining the rules to her. Satisfied she had a handle on it, he then announced it was time to play, but was astounded when I said, "Go ahead, but I'm not playing."

'My old work colleague came to my rescue (probably knowing I can be a bit feisty if I get riled) and said he'd rather sit around and have a drink. I would have gone home there and then if it weren't for the embarrassment his guests would undoubtedly have felt. So, when they left the next day, I gathered up all my things and was hard on their heels. He is still bombarding me with emails but he just doesn't understand my only explanation for the break-up – it just doesn't feel right any more – and I am ignoring them.

'So I was put off by a flower, a meal and a game of cards. But if you don't fancy them any more, you just don't!'

Why breaking up was the right thing to do

If someone is making you feel irrationally angry or physically sick to be near, then it is likely you're taking that out on them in some way. Consequently you may well not be treating them properly by staying with them.

The Repulsion can occur because they suddenly remind you of someone in your past or that you never really fancied them but just kidded yourself you did. It pretty much sounds the death knell and you've got to be honest about it.

How would you feel if someone held you in such little regard but kept up the relationship anyway? If you don't respect him, the sound of his voice constantly gets on your nerves and his mere touch makes your skin crawl, then you are doing the right thing by putting him out of his misery.

The sex was terrible

Who could forget the build up to Charlotte York's first knee-trembler with her dashing doctor fiancé Trey McDougal in *Sex and the City*?

Charlotte was utterly convinced that it would be magical and was even prepared to wait for her wedding night – but in the end it turned out to be the ultimate in anticlimaxes (quite literally) and it all went downhill from there for Charlotte and Trey.

As much as you can work at it, if something is fundamentally wrong (or off-putting), then there's no getting away from it.

Ann was really into her new man Mark and was convinced that there would be fireworks in the bedroom, but when it did occur, it was all a bit clumsy.

'For me, it was all a bit hit and miss,' she says. 'I just wasn't getting into it or feeling particularly comfortable, and I just couldn't relax because of the level of noise he was making. Each time, he'd let out a yelp or a groan. We're talking really loud!

'I'm not a prude, but I'm not very vocal either, preferring that sort of thing to remain between me and my man and not broadcast to my housemates, let alone the whole street!

'When I asked him if he could keep it down, he told me he couldn't. We tried a few times but I never felt fully comfortable. It was always going to be bad (too noisy) sex and, in the end, I just gave up.'

In another friend Olivia's case, she took an instant dislike to her new man's, err, little friend.

'I feel terrible about this but he just had a really odd one,' she reveals candidly. 'It was long and skinny and looked like a chipolata that had been left out to sweat in a warm kitchen, or a severed finger. I couldn't look at it without feeling mildly nauseous, which is terrible because in every other respect he was lovely. In the end, I had to call it a day, but I never told him why because even though I'm clearly a bad person, I'm not *that* bad.'

Why breaking up was the right thing to do

If we were to believe tabloid exposés, most people (or celebs and glamour girls at least) do it seven times a night, complete with sex toys and lots of swinging from the chandeliers.

While that all seems a bit OTT, in most new relationships it's true that you can't get enough of each other for the first few months, and then gradually it starts to fade. But if that lusty longing just isn't there at the start, it takes a very robust couple to cope with a sexless relationship. If it's early days and there's zero appeal, why put yourself through that? If the hot sex isn't there at the beginning, it's never going to happen, and it's probably best to move on.

A happy hangover with Transitional Man

Do you remember when hardly a day would go by without you seeing a picture in newspapers and magazines of Sienna Miller looking radiant on the arm of her boyfriend Rhys Ifans?

During that period Rhys (clearly knowing he was punching well above his weight) looked like the cat that had got the cream. But although Sienna too looked smitten for a while, it wasn't really any surprise that she soon broke it off.

Not long before she took up with Rhys, Sienna was dating oh-so-serious Jude Law. And prior to their split, the young actress was being fast-tracked to future wife and stepmother-of-four at the grand old age of twenty-two. But then Jude was alleged to have cheated with the nanny and the death knell began to sound.

They limped on for a while but then broke up, only for Sienna to find love and distraction with Jude's polar opposite – oh-so-boho Rhys. Funny guy Rhys unlocked the fun-loving Sienna, making her laugh and teaching her to be comfortable in her own skin – and it was probably just what she needed after such an intense time with surly Jude.

Suddenly, Sienna was confident and happy with a

boyfriend who adored her and helped her feel at ease with herself – but she wasn't ready to settle down yet.

Just as the engagement rumours began to circulate, Sienna bolted, leaving a heartbroken Rhys to search for answers in the bottom of his pint glass. But it wasn't personal, Sienna just needed to learn a bit more about herself and then spread her wings and fly. Rhys helped her with that – he was her Transitional Man.

Many of us have spent some period of our lives with a Transitional Man. He's the one who picked you up after you'd been knocked down. He's the love equivalent of bangers and mash on a cold day.

A friend, Matilda, opted for her Transitional Man after feeling neglected and put down in her last relationship – but she always knew the relationship had a shelf life.

'Being with Rob was like a happy hangover,' she says. 'You know when you've had a great night and the next day you're all cosy, lying on the sofa, eating crap food, watching TV . . . But that fuzzy feeling began to define the relationship, the walls were closing in on me. He loved me unconditionally but it was like a happy sedation. I knew that this wasn't right for me in the long term so eventually I decided it was time to get out and move on.'

Why breaking up was the right thing to do

In the beginning, he gave you the confidence to believe in yourself again. But while it was nice and warm and safe, deep down you knew that he wasn't The One.

Being with Transitional Man will ultimately make you feel bored and trapped because realistically you know you're not going to be together for life, yet he might have long-term expectations.

Staying too long in this scenario means you exist in a kind of no man's land inside your Transitional chap's comforting cocoon. It's time to spread your wings – and let him free too.

Opposites repel

It was Katherine Hepburn who said, 'Sometimes I wonder if men and women really suit each other. Perhaps they should live next door and just visit now and then?'

No one wants to go out with a clone of themselves, but if you are going to live together in peace and harmony, then there clearly has to be at least some common ground to move forward.

If romance does happen to blossom with your polar opposite, chances are that, at first, the stark differences in your opinions and values helped ignite sexual chemistry, with heated arguments leading to a fiery climax in the bedroom. But, after a while, having the same rows over and over can become very boring. If you are completely different in every way, then it's highly likely you'll end up disagreeing about just about *everything*. Then, the day inevitably comes when you'll wake up and realise you can't be bothered to say anything at all.

When Kay and Rick first met, their different opinions

about politics, education, careers and life in general created a passionate frisson between them. 'Rick was staunchly Labour where I was a bit of a Tory girl,' reveals Kay. 'We'd have big discussions about things, both our statements would get more and more outlandish, and he would wind me up a treat by calling me Kay Thatcher!'

But, after several months, it eventually got to the point where Kay realised that Rick was so addicted to one-upmanship that he'd happily argue black was white.

'It just got too tiring,' she says. 'I like a good debate but he left me exhausted. At first I found his boldness and fearless approach to arguing exhilarating and sexy. We'd agree to disagree and fall into bed. But I eventually realised he was, in fact, a complete arse, and in my view completely wrong about everything!'

Why breaking up was the right thing to do

You say to-may-to, I say to-mah-to – and we frigging hate each other!!

Fighting 24/7 will leave even the most provocative person tearing their hair out or collapsing in an exhausted heap. While a certain frisson can get the blood pumping, long-term love is built on foundations of mutual support and understanding – not wall-to-wall heated rows. Research has also shown that the most successful couples have more in common than not. If one of you has the sense to say, 'Let's call the whole thing off', be thankful that at last you finally agree on something!

Friendly fire

Introducing your boyfriend to your friends is a massive deal and also very nerve-racking. And, for most of us, it's a bit of a deal-breaker. If he can't charm those important people in your life, then things begin to turn a bit sour . . .

Felicity's ex-boyfriend, Nat, was a nice guy. He was artistic and kind, but very absorbed by his work. 'Everything else, including me, took a very second place,' she reveals. 'Perhaps because of this he found it extremely hard to remember my friends.'

As their relationship progressed, Nat's terrible face-recognition abilities became increasingly embarrassing, and were also very much noted by all of Felicity's friends.

'Every time we went out with them he would be very sweet and make sure he went around the room. He'd introduce himself to everyone with: "Hi, I'm Nat, you must be one of Felicity's friends. What's your name?" To which they would all reply (in an increasingly irritated fashion as the years went by): "What do you mean? We all went out last week!"

'Yet no matter how often he met them, a week later he would do exactly the same thing.'

Unsurprisingly, Felicity's friends assumed they were incapable of making any impression on him. 'Needless to say, they all thought he was really rude!' she adds. 'He isn't, though, he just can't see beyond what directly affects him. However, it did get very embarrassing and we eventually parted company.'

Poor Adele found herself in the opposite scenario. As much as she tried to crack her boyfriend's inner circle of female friends, the cliquy cluster never warmed to her.

'I could never figure out why, but Nathan's friends just hated me,' she says. 'They were all fashion students and, well, I wasn't.

To make matters worse, Nathan's closest friend and flatmate was a girl called Kirsten, who was also best friends with his two ex-girlfriends Eva and Jade. So I was shit out of luck from day one.'

Whenever Adele spent time with Nathan, she was dismayed to discover that Kirsten, Eva and Jade would inevitably be there. 'When I went to the flat they'd all be there, sitting on the sofa, drinking tea and giving each other knowing looks if I dared to speak,' Adele recalls. 'Eva and Jade often stayed the night, which when I wasn't there unnerved me. They'd also be at every party we attended, whispering in the corner like the Witches of Eastwick.'

When Adele first stayed over at Nathan's, she was surprised to discover that every morning Kirsten would come into Nathan's bedroom, without knocking, and bring him a cup of tea.

'Strangely, she never seemed to have the time to make one for me,' Adele adds. 'And she would happily sit on the side of the bed and wake him up for college! I WAS IN THE BED!'

When Nathan's birthday arrived, Adele thoughtfully booked a table for dinner and arranged to meet him at the restaurant at 7 p.m. Excited by the prospect of some much needed quality time with her chap, she got dressed up to the nines and arrived early for their reservation. But it was only after she'd been waiting for an hour that she discovered that her birthday treat for Nathan had been scuppered by Kirsten. She had organised him a surprise party and failed to alert Adele.

'I got a phone call from Nathan asking, "Where are you?"' she recalls. 'When I later asked Kirsten why she hadn't invited me, despite seeing me that very morning, she looked at me all wide-eyed and innocent and said, "Oops, I forgot." I didn't believe a word of it, but of course Nathan did.'

With Nathan listening to everything Kirsten said, Adele began to get increasingly frustrated. 'Whenever I said anything against Kirsten, he immediately took her side and told me I was just being paranoid.'

When Christmas arrived, Kirsten had another nasty little trick up her sleeve. 'We had a party at the flat and Kirsten was handing out really thoughtful gifts to everyone, like little books or trinkets. But when I unwrapped my present she'd bought me a Barbie doll. "It just reminded me of you," she told me, as Eva and Jade stifled their sniggers.

'Of course, Nathan said I should be flattered as Barbie was very pretty and he was sure that is what she was implying. What?'

The night Adele finally realised that Nathan would never support her over Kirsten was when they were all at a dinner party. 'After food and wine, everyone sat around in a circle and played a game where you chose the colour you thought the person next to you was. Nathan was red because he was fiery, bold and warm. Eva was green because she reminded the person next to her of the sea, and then all the guests one by one were described as bright colours for lovely reasons. I was the last person to be described – by Kirsten.

' "Oh, Adele is undoubtedly *beige*," she said, bold as brass. No one said anything and I just sat there blushing. The next day, Nathan and I broke up for good.'

Which brings us to a similar scenario with . . .

The parent trap

As the saying goes, you can pick your friends but not your family – but what it doesn't add is that you have even less choice about your nearest and dearest.

When it comes to the in-laws or a difficult, suspicious friend, diplomatic behaviour is often needed. But while most of us are prepared to invest in this, it's tempting to draw the line if you're not getting any support and your efforts appear to go virtually unnoticed.

For Stella, it was meeting the rather unwelcoming parents of her latest squeeze that really killed off their love affair.

'From the moment I travelled up north to meet Tommy's parents, it was clear they despised me, purely for being from down south!' she reveals. 'He was in the army and away from home so we had been dating a good six months before he took me back to Yorkshire to meet his parents.

'It turned out they had a deep distrust of southerners,

and within ten minutes of arriving, his mum accused me of putting on a posh voice because I thought I was better than them. They then spent the next hour telling my boyfriend about all the lovely single local girls who were dying to see him while he was home.

'He was clearly mortified and I didn't know what to do – I spent the next few days trying to build bridges with his mother, who openly said that I "wasn't his type" and should go back where I belonged.

'Tommy was clearly terrified of his parents and refused to stick up for me, so I left, utterly humiliated. I'm pleased to say that I've never encountered that kind of bigotry in Yorkshire again. I also heard that he eventually married a local girl who subsequently cheated on him. Bet his mother wasn't so keen on local produce after that!'

In a reverse situation, Sadie dumped her boyfriend Glen after taking him home to meet her parents. He was a good-looking lad from a nice family, but as Sadie soon discovered, behind the good-guy persona there was an obnoxious drunk just waiting to get out. He was pleasant enough to her parents but after a few beers he turned into a complete hooligan with a mouth like a sewer, lacing everything he said with the F and C words.

'The crunch came when he joined our family at an event in the village,' she reveals. 'By the end of the night my Dad was ready to take him outside for "a word". He was really very rude and arrogant both to my father and some of our family friends. Even my mates, supposedly more open-minded, were astonished at what an obnoxious little twerp he was.'

Why breaking up was the right thing to do

There is a difference between tolerating someone and being openly rude. While plenty of girls can take or leave their bloke's friends and plenty of families aren't exactly fans of their beloved boy's new girl, in polite society you make an effort.

If your fellow's family or friends are being positively vile, yet he is too lily-livered to stand up for you, then who wouldn't want to walk? It's all about respect and while it is understandable that he is keen to tow the line with those important people in his life, just sitting back and watching while you are treated badly is not on.

In a reverse scenario, if you are steadfastly loyal to your loved ones or pals and your man just won't put in the effort, then something has to give. After all, being in love isn't the be-all and end-all – you need your support system of friends and family too. If your man is refusing to embrace the whole package, then he simply isn't worth the bother.

No such thing as a harmless flirt

At some stage, we've all had friends who are clearly dating a bit of a sex pest. It's the boyfriend who you assume is totally into your lovely pal until he stares into your eyes just a little bit too long over polite conversation, or he finds it necessary to place his hands on your hips as he moves past you at the bar.

And he's the same philanderer who shamelessly checks

out the waitress while you and your friend try to pretend you haven't noticed.

Once, I was in a London nightclub when I saw a young man on the other side of the room smiling at me. For the next half an hour he kept looking over at me and grinning. Then he wandered over to introduce himself and offered to buy me a drink. He'd clearly had a few and as we made small talk made no effort to hide the lusty look in his eyes. He told me his name and we chatted for a while. It turned out he worked for a local brewery in their marketing office.

'Oh, my friend's boyfriend works there I think!' I exclaimed.

'Really?' he laughed. 'What's his name?'

'I'm not sure,' I replied. 'But the girl he's going out with is called Donna. Do you know her?'

Suddenly, there was an obvious physical reaction from him. His eyes looked startled and his face turned whiter than a sheet. 'Um,' he muttered after some time. 'She's my girlfriend.'

Now it was my turn to gawp at him, speechless. Then, as I took in the full horror of the situation, Donna's boyfriend made his excuses and scarpered.

Rather excruciatingly, following this unfortunate encounter, I bumped into the same man accompanied by an unsuspecting Donna on a fair few occasions. With an unspoken tension between us, we both played dumb and when Donna was around he appeared on his best behaviour.

I agonised over whether to say something but, in truth,

Donna and I weren't best friends, just kind of friends of friends. I didn't know her well enough for heart-to-hearts and I was scared of being branded a troublemaker. So I eventually decided it wasn't my place to rock the boat. After all, nothing had happened, and perhaps I should give him the benefit of the doubt and assume he was just very drunk?

And even if he did have a wandering eye, maybe Donna was deliberately ignoring her boyfriend's inner philanderer credentials and carrying on regardless?

A year or so passed and I discovered Donna was engaged. It made me feel weird but I kept my gob shut. Then, six months before the wedding, I heard that it was all off. Donna's boyfriend had left her for someone else.

I felt very, very guilty and vowed never to sit on the fence again. Now I stand by my belief that there is no such thing as a harmless flirt.

Another long-suffering friend, Fleur, had the patience of a saint while dating Nick, a man who made no attempt to disguise his wandering eye.

'He was always eyeing up other girls [nice] and even tried to chat up someone when I took him along to one of my friend's birthday parties!' she reveals.

'He had a very inflated view of his own attractiveness and I even saw him showing off to a young mum once. He was actually lying on his back doing bench presses by lifting her nine-year-old son off the floor one-handed. Can you believe I actually went out with this guy? What was I thinking!'

The breaking point came when Fleur caught Nick eyeballing a married girl from his office. 'I just stood there like an idiot watching them stare at each other,' she says. 'Then two weeks later I discovered a printed-out email from another girl at work telling him to go home, think about her and "play with himself"! You can imagine how I hit the roof and decided to end it after that.

'Now I just wish I'd saved myself the heartache and ditched him while he was just looking and not touching!'

Why breaking up was the right thing to do

Maybe I'm speaking out of turn, but I do think men can be fairly transparent when they are either up to – or thinking about being up to – no good. Occasionally, you meet a real master of deception, a pathological liar who hoodwinks everyone he meets but, more often than not, the womaniser signs are there, it just depends on whether you choose to see them.

First things first, if your beloved is really into you, then naturally he should spend the majority of his time eyeing YOU up – and not everyone else. I'm not suggesting all girlfriends should turn into the 'peek' police – cut the boy some slack to ogle if Kelly Brook walks into a bar – but leering at every woman he sees (including a passing nun flashing a bit of ankle) is just not on.

So, remember, if you ended it because he always seemed to have one eye on the door, then you had a very valid reason. After all, you've met the 'harmless flirt' in different guises before and you instinctively knew his real intentions. When he moved that bit closer, looking from your eyes to your lips and back again with a wry little smile, you knew exactly what was on his mind.

If your man is behaving that way to other women, it's likely they can read the signs too. As the traffic light, which should be on red, moves swiftly from amber to green, sooner or later he'll meet a lady companion who is happy to jump on board. (Incidentally, we'll be covering bona fide cheats in the next chapter.)

On a final note, most compulsive flirts do it because they need validation from women that they're attractive, so it's behaviour that almost certainly won't stop. In fact, it could actually get worse as he gets older.

The day time stood still

Sometimes, break-ups aren't at all dramatic. A love affair may fade over time and dwindle amicably. It can end by mutual agreement with an ongoing friendship. Other times, while the fireworks and nasty rows might not be there, an increasing disillusionment could be rumbling under the surface, especially if you feel your relationship is stuck in a boyfriend-shaped rut as he just won't commit.

When you started dating, wasn't Margaret Thatcher in power? Yet nothing has changed in your relationship. The country is in recession, power dressing is all the rage and he *still* hasn't moved in, let alone proposed. Over the years, you've been to precisely twenty-five weddings of close friends, been bridesmaid five times and gained eight godchildren.

Being with him felt comfortable and right, but after seven years it was clear that when it came to marriage and babies, you just weren't singing from the same hymn sheet.

For a long time you tried to convince yourself that you didn't really care, but were you really convincing anyone? In fact, deep down, that last christening was pretty torturous. You weren't imagining things when your girlfriends eyed you pitifully as you cooed over your friend's baby. And, yes, your bachelor boy was being patted on the back by all his under-the-thumb mates, like he was some sort of modern-day hero, courageously laughing in the face of your blatant broodiness.

But, in the end, you just knew – if he hasn't done the deed by now, he never would. So you called it a day . . .

Why breaking up was the right thing to do

There's no doubt relationships are difficult to predict. Over the years you change and grow (not always at the same rate). Suddenly, you might be salivating over baby booties in Baby Gap, while he still thinks downing a pint in under thirty seconds is a reason he shouldn't retire from the all-day drinking circuit just yet.

But if you're aching for a baby and imagining your egg supply shrivelling in your ovaries month by month, while he still thinks you have all the time in the world, then something has to give.

As difficult as the conversation about his 'intentions' is to have, it's better than carrying on with false hope. If he can't provide you with the assurances you know you need, then the credits are already rolling.

The bitter pill of success

A couple of years ago, an American report on family and marriage suggested that the risk of divorce rises when women out-earn their husbands. While it made depressing reading, sadly there are some men who cannot handle dating a career girl.

When Molly met John he had a high-flying career and she was just starting out. 'I was intimidated as he was older, very successful and, in my eyes, he could have anyone,' she says. 'I told him my ambitions and hoped that he would encourage and support me. I was a model girlfriend, trying to be thoughtful and loving and looking after my man, but I also had something to prove to myself. I wanted to make my family proud, pay off debts and do well.

'So, I worked hard at home and at work. The mistake I made was believing that he'd always love me for being me and that he wouldn't feel threatened by my drive and determination.'

Over the years of their relationship, Molly never lost sight of her ambitions and grafted hard to make a name for herself. But as she excelled and eventually began to earn more than John, she began to notice a change in his attitude towards her.

'I worked in advertising and when I told him excitedly about what I'd achieved, he'd reply with sneering put-downs. He'd say things like, "I can't believe you think that's good, our advertising company can get that at the drop of a hat every week." Or he'd give me the cold shoulder when I'd supported him with so many things. Every time he dismissed what I'd done, it felt like a blow to the stomach.

'When he told me I'd changed and that he'd loved the person I was before I worked so hard, that really hurt. I was still the same. I hadn't morphed into some weird *Devil Wears Prada* child-hating monster!'

In a painful irony, as Molly's career began to soar, John's began to flounder. 'I was paying half our mortgage in an overstretched situation he'd landed us in (God knows how he expected me to bake cakes *and* work nine to five). I just felt underappreciated while he seemed to feel neglected and threatened by my success. He just couldn't grasp that I was working longer hours to help us build a future together.

'It made me realise that sometimes there is no room for unconditional love. In John's eyes, I had to be the way I was when I first met him, or else.'

Why breaking up was the right thing to do

Everyone has the right to pursue their dreams, whether it's a rewarding life as a stay-at-home mum or navigating the cut-throat world of big business. But if your master wants you to stay at home, don a gingham pinny and bake cupcakes, and you want to cook up a storm in the boardroom – then things are about to get very hot in the kitchen.

As much as retrosexual men (chaps who long for a traditional set-up with a wife to greet them with a kiss on the doorstep and a hot, wholesome meal on the table when they arrive home) are allegedly making a comeback, career girls are still enjoying the buzz of making their mark.

If he resents your goals and aspirations and, even worse, puts your achievements down, where does that leave you? The alternative is giving it all up for a life of regret, just to appease the regressive instinct of your 1920s man. So it's no wonder that you couldn't stand the heat.

The curse of the kept man

While men can clearly feel that a successful girlfriend threatens their masculinity, the opposite can also be said. The murky waters of the dating pool can also be littered with hidden dangers, like slackers, scroungers and idle sods . . .

In another shocking tale of unashamed sponging, Simone lived for almost four years with Alex, a would-be screenwriter. 'He said I was the first woman he could imagine marrying or having children with (but didn't actually propose).'

When they met, Alex had his own business but soon decided he was not cut out for advertising, or work, and from then on did not earn any money.

'Three months after we met, his father died and he was grief-stricken, so I tried to be understanding,' reveals Simone. 'I thought it was a temporary setback, but it actually set the pattern for the rest of our relationship. I owned a house that had a large mortgage and that I paid for single-handedly.

'We were meant to have flatmates to help pay the rent but, instead, Alex moved in a friend. He failed to tell me that his friend had a raging cocaine habit, so neither of them ever paid any rent.

While I worked long hours, Alex would sit at home playing his guitar, drinking anything he could get his hands on, and supposedly working on his screenplay. He didn't do anything around the house, although when he occasionally cooked it was always a lavish gourmet dinner.

'Curiously, for someone who depended on others to support him, Alex only liked the best of everything and seemed to feel constantly disgruntled that he was having to slum it with me.

'I used to say that I didn't mind how humble his occupation was or even if he earned any money, but it was the slothfulness and inertia that made life so difficult. He just didn't do anything. Even if he had tended a vegetable garden or studied or done something useful I would have had more respect for him.'

As the months passed, Simone found it increasingly hard paying all the bills and keeping the show on the road. 'The final straw was when he invited a group of his friends to a restaurant and, after entertaining them, expected me to pick up the bill.

'Unbelievably, just after I ditched him, I found he had been having an affair for nine months with a girl from a coffee shop we used to go to together. He took great glee in telling me they had great sex and that she didn't wear mismatched old underwear.' Nice!

Why breaking up was the right thing to do

If you wanted a full-on dependent, you could have popped out a kid by now. But a man-child sponger was not what you'd bargained for and, in truth, you probably let him get away with it for far too long.

He's clearly old enough and ugly enough to support himself, and by allowing you to dish out the pocket money, he's taking advantage. You ditched him because bankrolling an ungrateful pauper does not a good relationship make.

Tightwad tensions

So the half man, half leech was swiftly, exterminated, but arguably an even worse 'sponger' hybrid is the one who pinches his own pennies away.

As a friend, Julie, puts it: 'Ever heard the one about the boyfriend who invited his new girlfriend away for a romantic weekend, booked a swanky hotel as a surprise, ordered champagne in the room, and then asked her to split the bill when they checked out? What an ARSE.'

Another pal, Karen, found herself in an equally disappointing situation when she copped off with a military officer.

'To be honest, he was a bit of a misogynist and didn't seem to have a high opinion of women,' she reveals. 'But it was the tightness that really got to me as I think it's one of the most unattractive traits, especially as I had been very generous to him.'

When Karen first met Rupert, it was clear he was pretty well off. He owned two homes, and was looking to buy another abroad.

'The first night I met him, we'd kind of been set up and were out with friends,' she reveals. 'I thought I would be generous and after my friends (but not him) had all bought rounds, I offered to buy the next. He feigned the whole "It's not your round", while not offering to buy the round himself. So I just bought it and proceeded to go home with him that night. At this point, all I was interested in was a one-night thing.

'But the next day, I was having friends over for Sunday lunch and he said he wanted to stay. So I agreed and we walked to Sainsbury's. As I filled a basket with food, he suddenly said quite firmly, in a military, no-nonsense way, "Bread. I need bread."

'So we went and bought bread. But when we got to the checkout he let me pay for everything, which was fair enough as it was my friends who were coming over, but he didn't even try and buy a bottle of wine or anything.'

Despite Rupert's tightness, Karen ended up seeing him for four months, forever hoping that he might actually put his hand in his pocket. 'Even though I cooked him dinner several times, he never once bought me wine or flowers,' she exclaims. 'There was even a time when I didn't have any money on me and I had to ask if it was OK if he bought me my cappuccino in a café. He answered "yeah" in that kind of "it's OK this time but don't ask again" tone.'

The final straw was when Karen and Rupert went for a pub lunch and, because he couldn't get any money out, she paid. 'He was really rude throughout the meal so, in the end, I stormed out,' she says. 'I didn't speak to him for the rest of the night and ignored all future calls. I'm not at all the type of girl who expects to have all her drinks and meals paid for – in fact, I go out of my way to go halves, but he expected to be treated like a king and pay for nothing.

'He's now with a waitress, which I think is perfect: she serves for a living and so she'll serve him, which is exactly what he wants!'

Why breaking up was the right thing to do

Seeing moths fly out his wallet when you know there's plenty of money stuffed under the mattress is pretty unattractive. If he looks constipated at the thought of spending even a tiny token of his hard-earned cash on you, then it's unlikely he'll show generosity in other areas, or change.

So picture a life of penny-pinching, sharing the bath-water and arguments over when to flush the toilet. While thriftiness is in fashion, being a tight git is not.

Worryingly, any one of us could find ourselves in the frightening situation of being involved with a man who wants to control or belittle us. When possessiveness, or any kind of abuse, is involved, the only positive outcome is when the victim finally feels able to leave it all behind.

One friend, Amy, experienced a classic example of how domestic violence can often start with psychological mind games. Thankfully, she found the courage to get out but reveals she still finds it very painful to talk about.

'I started dating a guy when I was in a pretty vulnerable place, and, boy, did he take advantage,' she says. 'Over the course of a year, he chipped away at all my self-confidence, criticising everything from my wardrobe to my driving, leaving me a shell of a woman, who believed I was stupid, ugly and lucky to have him because no one else would touch me.

'Looking back now, it's hard to imagine how this could have happened, but I know many other women who've been through it, and it's borne of possessiveness at its most sinister.'

As the relationship progressed, Amy wasn't allowed to go out without her boyfriend, and if she even spoke to another man, it was seen as flirting and he'd either explode with rage or ignore her for days.

'My every move was tracked, analysed and belittled,' she adds. 'Eventually, I found a shred of dignity and plucked up the courage to fight back, at which point he beat the crap out of me and broke my nose. I had the evil bastard arrested and never looked back.'

Another lovely girl, Zoe, had a terrible time at the age of seventeen when she dated a guy five years her senior.

'Johnny was a small-time drug dealer selling acid and the like, and he had a real hold over me,' she recalls. 'He didn't like me seeing my friends, was very intimidating and often took money from me. But it was only after I was arrested with him that I realised I was best off out of it.

'My parents, quite justifiably, hated him, but knew ultimately that leaving him was a decision I'd have to come to myself. He wasn't allowed across the threshold of their drive so we used to stay in his hovel of a rented room.'

Although Zoe tried ending it a few times, Johnny always persuaded her to stay. After numerous attempts to break things off, she finally decided to tell him she was moving to Nottingham to go to university. It seemed like a good get-out clause to end things once and for all.

'The night I broke it to him he was sitting in the bath, so I blurted it out and immediately headed for the door. But Johnny came flying out of the tub after me. He grabbed me at the front door, shouting that I couldn't leave him and that he loved me and always would. I struggled free, opening the front door, but he smacked me in the face, dislocating my jaw. Scrabbling up from the floor, I kicked him where it hurt and legged it.

'I headed home with a swollen face in a right state, and told my mum (but not my dad as I am sure he would still be in prison now for the injuries he would have inflicted on

Johnny). Mum bundled me into a car and took me to hospital, where I had to have my jaw shoved back into the socket.'

Afterwards, Zoe shed her tears in private. She was horrified that Johnny had hurt her but she'd been in love with him too. 'I just felt so worthless and confused,' she admits. 'Of course, my parents were nothing but relieved, but I felt very lonely. I had no friends to turn to, as over the six-month period of our relationship, Johnny had ensured I lost most of them – actually, pretty much *all* of them.'

Unfortunately, Johnny wasn't about to leave Zoe alone. About a week later, he turned up at the fish and chip shop where she worked, wanting to talk. 'As there were no other customers, I was pretty much a sitting duck, and the only way to get rid of him was to agree to meet him,' she says. 'So, when I finished my shift, I stupidly allowed Johnny to pick me up in his car and we went for a drive.

'He immediately started to get really irate and, not wanting to wind him up, I tried to be sympathetic to his feelings. As we drove round the town centre, I started crying, saying I was sorry, but at the same time trying to explain that I thought it was best if we parted now, as I was thinking of university.'

It was at that moment Johnny lost all control and started to accelerate. 'He just screamed at me, "If I can't have you, no one else will", then he drove the car straight into a brick wall, narrowly missing several people on the zebra crossing.

'I was convinced I was about to die. But, amazingly, the car was so old and big that it was surprisingly resilient. In the aftermath, I sat stunned in the car, crying with and my back killing me. The paramedics arrived and tried to calm me down, and all I could say over and over was, "My dad is going to kill me." I'd promised him I would never see Johnny again. But the ambulance man was really kind and told me that my dad would just be pleased I was all right.'

'At the hospital, I went through numerous tests and X-rays to find that I had a fracture in my lower back as a result of the impact,' Zoe adds. 'Johnny, on the other hand, had absolutely nothing wrong with him.'

For the next six weeks, Zoe endured a very wretched time, dosed up on strong painkillers and stuck in a hospital bed, flat on her back. 'I wasn't allowed to twist, bend or anything,' she says. 'I just had to lie flat. It was pretty miserable, to say the least.

'When my parents picked me up from the hospital, Johnny was actually waiting by their car to see me. I totally ignored him. Then, a few days later, a snapped wax heart was pushed through the letterbox with a poem, both of which went straight in the bin.

'So I mended myself, dried my tears and found some friends again – funnily enough, the real ones were always there, I just hadn't been aware of it. Then I went back to school and back to work. It took me a long time to rebuild my self-esteem after Johnny, but I did it. Finally, I was able to see I'd been very unlucky and the majority of men just aren't like that.'

Why breaking up was the right thing to do

We all know that feeling frightened or intimidated should not be what love is about but sometimes it takes a while for us to realise that's the situation we're in. When your self-esteem is low or you feel you are in love, it's tempting to settle for less than you deserve, but we all have the right to feel happy and to be ourselves in a relationship.

When I've spoken to women who have moved on from past abuse or domestic violence, they've all said the same thing: once they found the strength to leave, they never looked back. They are now able to enjoy life with a real spring in their step and their decision to leave has been empowering. They felt strong and in control and, above all, happy.

No explosive explanation

Finally, let's deal with just one last scenario to makes your brain ache. When, seemingly, there's no big explanation, either on his or your part, as to why you should be breaking up – but yet you are . . .

For years you got on great, and everyone always told you what a fantastic couple you were. There were mini-breaks and summer holidays and time spent as the best of friends.

But now it's over, prompted by you or him because it didn't 'feel right' any more. In truth, it's probably all manner of small things – idiosyncrasies or bad habits that have niggled away for a long time. Individually, these little things might seem trivial, but slowly they have mounted up, and you feel you're not as close as you used to be.

Or maybe the rot set in because of incessant arguing: the same points laboured over and over again, until you felt numb and had no idea what caused the conflict in the first place.

Equally, as much as you love each other, perhaps the attraction just isn't there any longer. You've not slept together for months on end and feel more like brother and sister?

Why breaking up was the right thing to do

Not all relationships end with a heinous crime or infidelity. Often, it's a lot less explosive. It could be a seven-year itch or thirty-something angst that leads to this sad scenario, but sometimes, even when you are incredibly fond of each other, you still drift apart or stop fancying each other.

If the spark has gone, if every attempt to understand each other's point of view has failed, and behind closed doors one or more of you is unhappy, then the relationship may have reached its conclusion. It's never nice to break a heart – especially one belonging to someone you've loved and respected for a very long time. But in many ways, it's quite dignified to let each other go.

So here you are, still standing and bearing your battle scars with defiance – the enemy identified and intercepted.

Whatever your break-up was like – whether it was serious, sad, funny, farcical, drawn out or you felt disarmingly indifferent – you've now identified why it happened, you're going to deal with it, and you're ready to start picking up the pieces.

3.

I hate you so much right now

So what happens when you've been through a break-up disaster of catastrophic proportions? You just move on, right? Forget the swine who did the emotional equivalent of holding you down and ripping out your heart with a blunt, rusty meat cleaver.

Well, unless the NHS start funding a procedure to permanently erase your ex from your memory (as in the film *Eternal Sunshine of the Spotless Mind*), sadly that's just not going to happen.

When you've been betrayed or dumped inexplicably, the chances of the ensuing days or weeks being pain-free are as likely as finding a four-leaf clover. BUT, rest assured, there's still hope – which, in your heart of hearts, you kind of knew already.

No doubt, your mum, your friends and a little voice within will all be labouring the point – that this period of mourning, desolation and despair is only a fleeting affliction blah, blah, blah . . .That just around the corner you'll find acceptance and happiness – but, like everything in life, you have to work to get it.

It's a bit like having braces fitted to your teeth. You need to endure the discomfort, embarrassing metalwork and possible lisp to come out with perfect, straight dazzlers the other side.

Likewise, you need to be prepared to ride the wave of sadness and see where it eventually leads you – hopefully to calmer waters and sunny climes. If you think about it, although the pain feels fresh and new, you've probably been here before (or you've seen friends experience it), so you know that sooner or later things do come full circle. You can and will feel contented once more. In a few months' time you may even be whooping with glee at how insignificant the man who broke your heart now seems.

At worst, by then, you'll probably feel a small pang of nostalgia or sadness as is normal. But it's likely you'll also be able to laugh and joke about your evil ex. Hell, you might even share your story in a comical fashion like all the lovely ladies in this book!

Either way, you are ultimately going to end up feeling very proud of yourself. You took the pain, it didn't break you and you came out the other side stronger, happier and empowered. After all, getting through life's low points is what enables us to savour those highs.

So, without further ado, let's set off on the road to recovery . . .

Comfortably numb

When your beloved boyfriend has been the closest person to you, whether for three months or five years, suddenly being forced to face the music may seem incomprehensible.

If the break-up was thrust upon you like a bolt from the blue, being on your own can seem frightening and unfathomable. So, immediately facing up to the grim reality of your situation and going cold turkey might be unrealistic. Instead, after the initial shock and probable tears, the denial route can be a much more appealing option.

When faced with such adversity, who could blame your brain for doing the equivalent of what squirrels, and other cute mammals, do in the winter – hibernating until the frosty front has disappeared? Sometimes, we do just instinctively departmentalise – putting some of those raw emotions into a box to be dealt with later (although what goes in must come out again).

Most likely, you will be up and down like a yo-yo as your thoughts veer dangerously close to the daunting reality of your heartbreak, but then quickly retreat to the fuzzy fantasy realm your psyche has created to protect you from a total breakdown.

The logical part of your brain may be shouting at you to face facts, but the emotional side will be hollering too: 'Don't give up! There's always hope!' And at this point you may find yourself uttering one of the following sentences:

'Maybe we could have an open relationship?'
'I don't think he meant to make a pass at his secretary.'
'He can't help being a sex addict.'
'He just needs some time to think and find himself.'
'He's doing it for me, really.'

'He doesn't love her; she just got him drunk.'
'She's ugly; they'd have ugly kids; he'll come back.'

Consequently, you will need really patient friends. Over the next few days you are about to unleash the biggest deluge of verbal diarrhoea on them and a suspiciously skewed recollection of past events.

But who could blame you? When you are hit by the fear of suddenly being on your own, that panic can leave you stabbing blindly in the dark for some kind of get-out clause.

You might do or say anything to find a glimmer of hope for your flat-lining romance – even taking the blame in some way for his misdemeanours. But while your friends may politely listen for a certain amount of time, you can't really expect them to be as blindly optimistic as you are or to bite their tongue indefinitely.

When you've seen your best girl pal pooped on from a great height or hurt badly by a less-than-noble suitor, it takes all the diplomacy of the United Nations not to wade straight in there with some ugly home truths.

Which is why your well-meaning and protective friend may suddenly get a militant look in her eye and unleash a damning sermon about your ex. Don't get angry with her – she's only got your best interests at heart. Somewhere in the ether, all her preaching – about how you deserve better, he was selfish and nasty or a lying little shit – may strike a chord with you. You might even meekly agree, while pretending to look equally indignant but, in truth, you're probably not really focusing – or listening.

Nope, you are actually replaying the syrupy scene on the seafront in Brighton last summer. The one where you pout coquettishly as he tries to steal your raspberry ripple ice cream.

You're probably finding it hard to focus on the cold bare facts because right now you need a bit of comfort, the chance of a positive outcome. You might even lie to your friend, claiming, 'I know it's over! I'm going to move on.' But that's just what we tell friends to pacify their concerned looks when they've taken the trouble to offer advice.

When your lovely friend has listened to your sobbing all the way through the penultimate episode of *Mistresses*, you know you need to give something back: words to show your inner strength and to prove that you are waking up and smelling the coffee.

But the minute such finite words come out of your mouth, it's probable that a hot flush of panic engulfs you. At which point you may sneak off and secretly text him, even though you know it's just prolonging the misery. The problem is that getting over someone isn't like flicking a switch.

Although there may be moments where you begin to see the light, the prospect of all hope being lost – a gloomy world where you will never get to snuggle up on the sofa next to someone special again, him clipping his toenails, you picking the remains of your dinner out of your teeth – is daunting. No wonder you need to go into preservation mode, kidding yourself that there's a tiny beacon of light at the end of the dark, dismal tunnel.

You need that secret hope in your heart that he'll be

back and sorry – and not out with his mates, ogling strippers and sinking beers in celebration of his return to bachelorhood.

Unfortunately, though, denial can only be a temporary state of mind. Sooner or later the full power of your break-up is going to slap you hard in the face and you need to hit rock bottom before you can clamber back up again.

Weeping, wrath and ruin

There comes a time when your sad little brain starts to stir. The fog of your hibernation period is lifting and reality bites hard.

Years ago, a relationship came abruptly to an end for me when I discovered my gorgeous boyfriend had cheated on me with a girl he met at a party.

The morning after the fateful night I awoke to a feeling of total despair. I lay in bed, too bewildered to cry properly, my tired mind desperately seeking impossible scenarios where everything would be OK again. But slowly and surely, the horrific truth began to hit me and my whole body began to throb with despair.

The Fear – an overwhelming feeling of foreboding, panic and misery – was about to hit me head on. I could feel it coming, a crescendo of pain moving up my body like a contraction. My heart was pounding in my chest and my throat felt constricted.

I tried pacing the room, but nausea hit me. I headed to the bathroom and tried unsuccessfully to be sick. Then I gripped the side of the sink, my whole body rigid and ears ringing, as I tensed and dug my fingernails into the ceramic. For a minute or two my throbbing digits detracted from the stabbing pain in my heart but finally, back in my bedroom, I succumbed and wept myself into oblivion.

With the floodgates firmly open, I thought I'd never stop. Eventually my caterwauling got so bad that I completely forgot to breathe and, blue in the face, shocked myself into momentary silence.

Summoning up all the energy I could muster, I managed to brush the mountain of snotty tissues from my bedspread, force myself up and switch the radio on. I had hoped an uplifting song might give me the boost I required to pull myself together. Unfortunately, it appeared I'd inadvertently tuned into the station's daily 'slit your wrists' segment. In the worst possible timing, the opening bars of 'Un-break My Heart' by Toni Braxton trickled out of the wireless and my howling peaked to a whole new level.

Unable to cope with anything more challenging than bawling, eating (handfuls of Crunchy Nut Cornflakes straight from the packet) and basic toilet functions, I battened down the hatches and returned to bed.

Several hours of sobbing later, I was pretty sure I could hear my housemate muttering profanities next door. Some people are all heart, aren't they? Didn't he understand that I *alone* was setting a world record as the most heartbroken, betrayed young lady since time began? No one else could possibly feel my pain. That was it. I'd never recover. I really was destined to be sad, lonely, finished, washed up – all at the age of twenty-one.

The following day, after a night of feverish and broken sleep, there was little improvement – although I had now combined weeping with a blistering rage. When you reach the anger stage and a rumbling resentment sets in, you tend to look a wee bit crazy – think Jack Nicholson in *The Shining*. Your eyes are sore and swollen and all you can think about is how he broke your heart and doesn't care.

You find yourself pacing the room, grinding your teeth and grimacing – half scornful, half smile – as you know you are not even remotely in control of your emotions.

Worryingly, if the evil little philanderer knocked on the door right now and declared his undying love for you, you'd probably jump on him and head straight upstairs. You hate yourself for being weak, you hate him for doing this to you – yet you love him.

And so the merry-go-round continues.

In my case, after veering from denial, to sobbing, to anger – not to mention almost inciting murder (my own at the hands of my housemates) – over several post break-up days, I wasn't about to give up my mournful despair.

At this point no one had actually told me what they were all thinking: 'We know you didn't deserve it, but stop being such a drama queen.' That is until, not at all self-indulgently, I chose to relive the heartache on the phone to my mum (for seemingly the millionth time in recent days), revealing how earlier I'd been slumped on the bathroom floor sobbing into the shag pile.

'That was a bit dramatic, wasn't it?' she finally remarked. 'Why don't you have a shower, then go outside, get some fresh air and I'm sure you'll feel much less sorry for yourself.'

I suddenly became very sulky on the phone – but only because she'd hit the nail on the head. Yes, I was hurting, but deep inside there was a wee bit of me slightly wallowing in the drama of being a wronged woman.

There was no doubt it was a shock initially, that I felt battered and bruised, but why was I so sure that getting over my rat-faced ex just wasn't an option? Did I actually prefer to stay cooped up, stewing in my own gloom and dribbling spittle and snot into the carpet? Immediately, I made a mental note to self that I would try not to be quite so pathet . . . err, dramatic from there on in.

I had a shower, washed my disgusting greasy hair, got dressed and headed outside to be blinded by daylight. Unbeknown to me – I hadn't opened my curtains since tragedy struck – it was a gorgeous sunny day. So I walked to Woolies, when it was still alive and kicking, and bought myself some magazines and a couple of CDs. I immediately felt better.

As usual, Mother did know best.

Not so long ago, a friend wisely told me a little trick you can do if you're ever feeling hard-done-by.

'Imagine there was a flash of light,' she said. 'And suddenly everything was gone – your friends, your family, your nice home, everything – and you're just lying there, with nothing. Now imagine there's another flash and suddenly you have it all back. How happy and grateful would you be?'

She's right. Shit happens and if you really think about it,

you usually find that things could be so much worse. Granted, it would take me a fair few months to mend my broken heart – but the best thing I ever did was cut out the woe-is-me crap, shrug off the inner masochist causing me to wallow and actually attempt to get over it.

Battling your inner masochist – phase one

1. I don't want to wash myself, my hair or apply make-up.
2. I will wear loose, dowdy clothing, preferably with an elasticated waistband.
3. I want to eat crap food and drink too much booze.
4. I want to torture myself by texting, calling him or spying on him on Facebook.
5. I am going to listen to mournful songs on repeat.
6. I am going to watch cheesy films and cry at the sad and happy bits – and spot all the 'hidden meanings'.
7. I will not see my friends.

OK, let's go through them one by one. Why is it that during that initial break-up period we seem so content to let our personal hygiene standards fall to the extent we look and smell like Great Uncle Bulgaria's dishevelled she-beast sister?

Because we can't really be arsed to help ourselves, that's why. But come on, there's a sensible lady in there somewhere. Just getting in the shower or soaking in the bath will not only remove the grimy, salty residue of tears clogging up our pores (and thus ward off pimples) but it is also a step towards feeling cleaner, healthier, happier and stronger.

Plus it is a fact universally acknowledged that when you have not bothered to wash, your hair is greasy and lank and you have been crying for hours, you *will* look at your worst. All you will see in the mirror is a very ugly, blotchy, she-troll with eyes like piss-holes in the snow. And how is that going to make you feel? Funnily enough, like a miserable, ugly she-troll.

The best thing you can do is dig out all your best pampering products – body scrub, exfoliating face wash, face pack, shea butter hair mask, deluxe body lotion – and get busy in the bathroom. Shave your legs, pluck your eyebrows, cut your toenails and paint them. Maybe even apply a bit of fake tan.

Yes, I know it's what's inside that counts (and we'll work on that too) but indulging yourself and going for an all-over cleanse is a good start. Finish off by blow-drying your hair and putting your slap on. There's no need for fake eyelashes and glitter mascara at this point but a bit of blusher will help give the impression you have returned to the land of the living.

Now, with your preening complete, don't even think about putting those stinky Winnie the Pooh pyjamas back on. 'But pyjamas are perfect!' I hear you say. 'There's no point getting dressed unless absolutely necessary.' Well, seeing as you've just made the effort to do your make-up and hair, how hard would it be to find a pair of jeans and a nice top?

With that sorted, it's time to consider your diet. Forget

ice cream, chocolate and booze – let's look at it practically. While a little of each won't do you any harm, bingeing on them is only going to make you feel bloated and depressed.

When you are going through a traumatic situation, your body needs to work extra hard to fend off colds and infection, so it is essential you feed it properly. Biscuits, ice cream, chocolate or booze may give you a short-term high but they are lacking in the essential goodness you need, and can also leave you feeling sick, headachy, wired or tearful.

Instead, you need to get outside, get some fresh air (see, I'm my mother's daughter) and arm yourself with the following:

Your break-up survival kit

Fresh fruit – fruits such as blueberries and bananas are good mood-boosters. Decent comfort food with vegetables – a good shepherd's pie served with broccoli, a wholesome leek and potato soup, or, if you really crave bangers and mash, have them with greens!

Rescue Remedy – Aha! The little yellow bottle of amazement! This little beauty contains a combination of flower remedies which, when sprayed on your tongue, help to ease feelings of anxiety, panic and loss of control. Not convinced? Well, it contains a tiny bit of booze too, so get stuck in.

Calming tea – When I was little I didn't sleep very well, so Mum gave me chamomile tea to help me relax and it really helped. I still drink it by the bucketload now. You have to get used to the taste but it's pretty inoffensive. If chamomile doesn't appeal, then there are various types of calming tea around containing anything from lavender to cocoa beans. Believe it or not, almost every housemate I've lived with has gone away an herbal tea (and potato waffle) convert – it's addictive!

A hot water bottle or teddy bear or both – yes, I know you're not eight, but you'll probably find those first few nights without him quite lonely, so cuddling up to something soft and warm will help.

A lavender cushion or aromatic oil – you can usually find these in the gift section of department stores or health food shops. Lavender is very calming and is great to put in the bath before you go to bed. Put the cushion or oil on your pillow within snorting distance to help you beat The Fear in the wee small hours.

Now for the next three points: calling, texting or spying on him; listening to Magic FM (as one friend says, 'As much as I love that station, it should be banned in a break-up scenario'); and watching sad bastard films. Why are you compelled to do it to yourself?

So call him umpteen times until he shouts at you or says something horribly cutting that you didn't want to hear. Stalk him on Facebook, stalk his friends, and keep on pushing and pushing until you find something you didn't really want to know.

Watch *The Break-Up* and despair at the parallels between Vince Vaughn and Jennifer Aniston's destructive on-screen relationship and your own former romance.

All these actions will result in just one thing – more tears before bedtime. And combined with all of the above, you are heading for full-blown hysteria before the day is through.

Susan learnt the hard way: 'After my most recent break-up, I spent a painstakingly awful two weeks indulging deluded thought processes that if I were to email or text him constantly, then he would realise what he was missing.

'Predictably, every time it ended in tears, and after a particularly bad, drunken texting session, where I might as well have proposed, I knew that I had to stop embarrassing myself, so the next morning I made some brave decisions.

'First, I deleted his number, erased him from my Facebook friends and told myself that I couldn't contact him for a whole month. Then I made a list of his bad points and stuck it on my wall. Below that I started a tally for every day that I didn't contact him.

'Whenever I felt lonely or missed him I would take a look at his bad list and remind myself how far I had come. I'm currently on day twenty-nine and feel so much better for not contacting him.'

We could all learn a thing or two from Susan's iron resolve. But it's undoubtedly hard, which is why at times like this you *cannot* ignore your friends. They are calling and trying to help because they have been through this at some time too. They know what it's like to want to cocoon yourself away, but they also know that the best thing you can do is get out there and distract yourself.

No one expects you to be the life and soul of the party, and you'll probably still want to cry when you get home. But, by battling your inner masochist, you'll be surviving rather than sinking – and will certainly be a lot nearer to recovery than the she-troll who was staring back at you from the mirror this morning.

So now you're well on your way to recovery, it's time to reiterate the facts. Since the days of Adam and Eve people have faced heartache and rejection – and survived.

Feeling heartbroken is not an elite affliction, you don't need a special membership and you don't have the exclusive rights to feeling melancholy and dejected.

You are now firmly enrolled in Broken Heart Boot Camp and it's time for some serious show-and-tell therapy.

It's just you, me and my mistress!

Let's start with the story of a young lady called Kerry who experienced one of the most gut-wrenching break-ups known to womankind – discovering the love of your life has a floozy on the go.

Kerry met Dom at university and three years of heady romance soon flew by. But once their studies ended, keeping up a long-distance relationship wasn't nearly as idyllic. Eventually, after twelve months of traipsing back and forth, Kerry decided that moving to Dom's home town was the only answer. So she packed up her life and moved to Reading.

Without friends and family nearby, and an ample commute to London with her new job at an advertising firm, Kerry accepts that she was hardly a barrel of laughs by the time she got home at 9 each night. But still, did that really give Dom an excuse to have an affair with – in Kerry's own words – 'his far from stunning, ginger boss'.

'I swear this isn't a case of me being bitchy,' Kerry insists. 'The witch that stole my man was a foot taller than me, two stone heavier and a dead-ringer for Princess Fiona from *Shrek*.'

Leading up to the point when she discovered Dom's betrayal, Kerry felt that her boyfriend seemed distant and that something was wrong. After weeks of discussions in which Dom remained pretty much mute about their relationship, Kerry decided to stay with a friend in London for a week to give him some space.

'To miss me, of course!' she says. If only.

Just a few days into their time apart, Kerry received a text from a mystery number. It kindly informed her that Dom was having an affair with a colleague at work, and that the anonymous texter 'thought she should know'.

An hysterical Kerry swiftly made her way out of the office at lunchtime and hot-footed it back to Reading to confront her cheating boyfriend. When she arrived, the flat was empty but she immediately spied a bottle of white wine in the kitchen (Dom only drank red) and two wine glasses by the bed. Turning detective, she scoured the sheets for evidence, which she found in abundance.

'This girl clearly had a severe moulting problem, as her long, greasy ginger hairs were all over my *my* white bedsheets,' reveals Kerry. Ouch.

The next piece of incriminating evidence came in the form of a mascara-sodden tissue that Kerry plucked from the side of the sofa. 'I later found out she had used this to dry her tears when Dom told her he didn't want to be with her and wanted to stay with me – hence the tactical "anonymous" break-us-up text she'd sent me earlier that day,' adds Kerry.

When Dom drove back to the house a good few hours later, his mistress wasn't far behind. His bit on the side's plan was to sit silently in the dark and watch as the drama unfolded. But when Dom pulled into the car park and torrential rain battered down, an eagle-eyed Kerry saw a car with a red-headed occupant driving in behind him. She barked, 'Go and get her then, she'll be getting wet out there!'

Seeing Kerry, his mistress sprung out of the car and headed towards the flat. A heated debate unfolded as she showed Kerry the loving texts Dom had sent her while he sat ashen-faced on the couch.

Not wanting to hear another word, Kerry quickly packed her belongings into a taxi. 'It cost me a hundred pounds from Dom's house to my mate's place in London but it was worth every penny,' she says.

Admirably, Dom's betrayal left Kerry crushed but not kaput. 'After he took me to hell and back, I got myself together and moved on,' she reveals. 'I channelled my energy into my career and bagged my dream job. Then, with my newfound happiness at work, I found the courage and confidence to go out again with my friends, dress up, and accept the offers of dates. I never spoke to Dom again and leaving him was the best thing I ever did.'

Our next betrayed young lady, Verity, was just twenty-two when she took a job for a design company and was instantly taken with her very hip and handsome twenty-five-year-old boss.

'Ronan was an incredibly smart, wealthy, yet generous guy and I couldn't believe my luck when he asked me out,' she recalls. 'Things progressed quickly and after six months we moved into an amazing penthouse flat. Ronan also showered me with gifts, including my own racy convertible. We were ridiculously happy too and all my mates thought I had the perfect life.'

But two years into their relationship, things started to sour. 'Ronan worked insane hours, and I was getting the hump with it,' she says. 'We were working it out but I decided to go on a four-week holiday to Malaysia with two mates to give us some space. Ronan saw me off at the airport saying we could work things out and that he would miss me. But whenever I called from Malaysia, I could tell something was wrong.'

Yet, when Verity returned home, Ronan was a changed man. 'He couldn't do more for me,' she says. 'Nothing was too much trouble. He told me he'd missed and loved me so much. I was like "Wow – I should have done this ages ago!"

'I did notice that some of my things, such as photos and toiletries, had been moved around a bit. When I asked, he said the cleaner had done a massive spring clean so I thought nothing more of it.'

Everything was going just fine until one night, out of the blue, Ronan's ex-girlfriend turned up at the flat while they were entertaining friends.

'Ronan just ushered her quickly into the hallway while I stayed in the lounge with our guests,' says Verity. 'It was all very odd. So later I confronted him about how she knew where the flat was. He then confessed that while I was away, they had met up for dinner a couple of times and that he'd brought her round to see the flat!

'Of course I was less than impressed by this revelation, but he said he was sorry, assured me nothing was going on, that he loved me. He also claimed that because they were childhood sweethearts they wanted to remain friends. He seemed so earnest, and because things were great between us, I gave him the benefit of the doubt.'

Life with Ronan continued to be good until three months later when he went away on business and Verity invited her sister to stay for a few nights.

'We always had loads of gadgets lying around the place, and one afternoon my sister picked up one of Ronan's old mobiles,' she recalls. 'She was playing around with it and asked why he had taken photos of our bathroom. Confused, I took the phone and stared at the pictures. Suddenly, the full horror of what he'd done hit me.

'Stored on his phone were reels and reels of photos of everything that belonged to me in the flat – toiletries in the bathroom, perfumes on my dressing table, photos of us both, body lotions on my bedside cabinet. Suddenly a horrible thought entered my head – had Ronan taken the photos so he could hide all my stuff and bring his ex to the flat?

'As the realisation of all this hit me, I dropped the mobile and dashed to the kitchen, where I threw up in the sink.'

When Ronan arrived home that night, Verity tearfully confronted him. While at first he denied it, he eventually admitted that all her suspicions were true. He confessed that he'd initially met up with his ex as friends, but confused by the feelings spending time with her had stirred up, he'd dated her the whole month Verity was away – and slept with her several times. In a callous, premeditated plan, he'd cleared the flat of Verity's belongings, met his ex for dinner, brought her to the flat and shagged her, in their bed, assuring her the whole time he was single.

He'd then meticulously replaced all Verity's belongings before she came home so that she'd be none the wiser.

'He insisted that it made him realise how much he loved me, that he didn't have any feelings for her, and that he wanted to be with me,' Verity explains. 'I was so devastated and torn, but I did actually believe him. We'd been getting on so well since I'd got back from my holiday, and his sudden change of attitude was now fully explained – a hundred per cent pure guilt.

'I took a deep breath – our life together was great and I loved him and knew he loved me too. So I pledged that I could forgive him – for what in my eyes was the most immoral of all sins – on the condition that he never saw or had any form of communication with her again. He accepted.'

Another three months passed quickly, and although Ronan, eager to make the most on his second chance, was devoted and steadfast in his feelings, Verity wasn't.

'I was living in a constant state of paranoia,' she admits. 'I regularly checked his mobiles or emails when he left his laptop on. I couldn't find anything incriminating but always had that nagging feeling at the back of my mind when he was "working late" or "out with the guys".

'In the end, I decided I couldn't live like that any more. I didn't like the sort of person I'd become, so reluctantly I left him.'

Over the course of their relationship Verity's friends had assumed she'd had a charmed life, but when she parted from Ronan it wasn't the trappings of luxury and wealth that she missed.

'Giving up the fast cars, exotic holidays, fancy restaurants and midnight speedboat trips up the Thames weren't, contrary to popular belief, the hardest part of my decision,' she says. 'Money may make the world go round, but it certainly cannot buy you happiness.'

'Ronan was my first love, the first man I'd lived with and an important part of my life for just over three years. He was someone I trusted and depended upon and who had made me so happy. Two years on, I'm still single.

'My confidence has been knocked when it comes to dating, so apart from a few flings here and there, there's been nothing serious. For the time being, I'm contented as I am. The only loves in my life are my running trainers and yoghurt-coated raisins.'

You could hardly blame Verity for being cautious when it comes to future affairs of the heart. But while she will be wistful that things went so wrong, one thing she won't ever regret is breaking it off with Ronan. It was his decision to compromise what could have been an amazing future. And his actions left her with no choice.

Sometimes relationships do recover from an affair – it all depends on why it happened and whether you are prepared genuinely to forgive. But if you have chosen to break it off with a love cheat, just remember why you did it: because the trust had gone; he betrayed and humiliated you; and because the philandering little toss-biscuit is clearly incapable of keeping it in his trousers.

How to spot a cheat – your essential guide from the poor souls they cheated on

'He started putting his phone on silent but paid it much more attention than usual.'

'You know he's probably cheating when he suddenly turns from the tramp you've come to know and love into the man you first met, working out, paying attention to his hair, making sure he smells good by covering himself top to toe in aftershave.'

'There's the old body language stuff that tells you he's being shady or lying – covering his mouth when speaking, rubbing or scratching his nose . . .'

'Overreacting to simple questions like "Did you have fun last night?" with responses such as "For God's sake, why are you always checking up on me."'

'Not answering the phone and vagueness about where he's been.'

'Changing the duvet cover in the middle of the day or week – when you normally do it weekly on a specific day.'

'Look inside the lid of his deodorant – that's where my cheating ex stashed his condoms. I was on the pill!'

"He buys you flowers for no reason – except to ease his conscience.'

'Taking his phone with him *everywhere*. I had a cheating boyfriend who took his phone to the loo and when he was running a bath.'

'My boyfriend was never a great timekeeper but suddenly "I'll be half an hour" meant three hours later.'

'I noticed that his parents were being friendly but in a really shifty way because they knew and felt awkward, and he suddenly didn't want me to see his friends.'

'He got texts at funny times of the night and was usually too tired to shag properly. Not that I'm bitter or anything.'

'When a random girl pops up on his Facebook as a new friend, you can be pretty sure he's shagging her, or trying to. Both happened to be the reality with my wanker ex.'

Whether cheating is involved or not, being on the receiving end of a break-up is vile. Your reintroduction to single life might be presented in the most gentlemanly of ways, but ultimately it still smacks of rejection.

My fate was once sealed over a lunch date, when my suitor dumped me somewhere between my chicken risotto and chocolate sponge pudding. As I put down my fork to listen, a sense of anger and injustice overwhelmed me.

'What?' I asked.

As he bravely repeated his statement, I screwed up my face with contempt and even stamped my foot like a petulant child.

'I'm sorry, Charlotte, but I'm not changing my mind,' he finally told me bluntly.

So I grabbed my coat and bag and stropped out of the restaurant.

But what on earth was I really complaining about? He didn't cheat on me; he didn't keep me hanging on. He had the guts to tell me the way it was. And, really, I should have counted myself lucky that he actually bought me lunch.

It could have been so much worse, as Nessie will demonstrate . . .

When happily settled girlfriend Nessie first ran her eyes over her fiancé's huge phone bill, the money he'd stacked up was the least of her worries. Instead, she was concerned about one particular mobile phone number that Don, her intended, had been calling several times a day.

Next, an email she really shouldn't have seen, but which Don had rather foolishly left on Nessie's laptop, confirmed what she most feared – her beloved was having an affair.

'We were about to move house together and suddenly everything was turned upside down,' Nessie recalls. 'It was such a betrayal that forgiving him just seemed impossible. So I was left with a week to find somewhere to live, my heart broken and my pride in tatters.

'To my utter dismay Don immediately started seeing the "other woman" and I later discovered he'd been telling everyone we knew that I'd treated him badly so his cheating would look justified!

'The way he behaved was very hurtful but ultimately got me through it. In the end, it showed me that I was better off without him, as he clearly wasn't a very nice person.'

So good riddance to Don the doughnut.

Next in our hall of shame is Stephen, who had evidently been wishing to break up with his girlfriend for quite some time.

The unfortunate young lady, Annabel, was some years his junior, very smitten and unable to grasp hints that he wanted out. So, after a few too many pints, spiteful Stephen turned up at her home and threw a book at her called *How To Be Single*. Ouch.

Then there was Annie, who viewed her cheating ex-fiancé as pretty despicable – until she hacked into his email and discovered an even worse revelation.

'It was bad enough he cheated on me,' she says. 'But then a few months later I couldn't resist logging into his email account. I immediately discovered that he had nearly married the girl he cheated on me with – while he was engaged to me!

'I was in shock for about an hour, but in the end I was pleased I'd done it. It made me realise what a lucky escape I'd had and I went back to feeling glad she'd taken the loser off my hands.'

Feeling better about your last break-up yet? No? He must have been a particularly wretched wrong-un. Well, let's move on to our next dastardly ditcher . . .

Joan is the first to admit that when she started dating Gary she knew he was a complete tosser – but love, as they say, is blind.

'He was totally in love with himself, selfish and fickle,' she reveals. 'Nevertheless, I carried on regardless. But after a while I had good reason to believe that not only was Gary appallingly vain but he was actually sleeping with people behind my back. So I called him and ended it over the phone.'

But Gary had never been dumped before and it knocked him for six. Indeed, so shocked was he that he drove through the night for two hundred miles to plead with Joan.

'When he arrived on my doorstep, all blotchy-eyed and insistent that he had done no wrong, I felt my resolve beginning to wane,' she admits. 'Reluctantly, I agreed that we could work things out but explained that he couldn't stay the weekend as I had a big night with friends planned. I waved him off in the hope of new beginnings and started to get ready for my evening out.'

Dressed up in her glad rags and make-up all applied, Joan was just about to leave the house when the phone rang – it was Gary.

'In a confessional outpouring which would surely have made a priest weep, he admitted that he'd been sleeping with his housemate behind my back, oh and his ex-girlfriend, and a girl from work – so funnily enough, he couldn't really carry on seeing me! Consequently my big night out was over before it even began.'

The brutal break-up hall of shame

'My ex dumped me by voicemail on New Year's Eve. I'd actually been in his car half an hour previously and he'd said, "I'll call you tomorrow and we can hang out." Thinking everything was fine, I headed home, changed to go out and celebrate with my friends. Then I found the message – GUTTED. My evening was ruined. I went out, couldn't handle it and left early. I spent the stroke of midnight crying on the Northern Line.'

'My boyfriend's ex called up when we were visiting my parents in Nottingham – she'd broken into his house to rifle through his address book to get the number! I was gobsmacked when she said we should have a lesbian affair – and that she'd break me in gently with a cinema date first! I promptly told her she needed to get help and put the phone down on her. The reason she was so nuts? It turned out my boyfriend was cheating on her with me!'

'When I phoned my boyfriend to tell him I'd found out my stepdad was dying, he said he'd be round straightaway, but turned up five hours later. It later transpired he was seeing his other girlfriend off at the airport.'

What an appalling bunch of cads and bounders. It's really no wonder that their victims still feel indignant. Falling in love means giving yourself to someone one hundred per cent and letting down your guard in the hope that they will treat you right.

When you have allowed yourself to be that vulnerable, it's an absolute blow to the stomach to find out that the person you love has betrayed you. Then finding the strength to leave takes real courage – as does giving up the ghost after a long and painful break-up. But if you've got this far, keep going!

There will always be times when it seems that the safer option is to go back to the comfortable folds of your relationship and kid yourself that somehow you can relive the glory days.

But if that means returning to someone you'll never trust again and a lifetime of feeling paranoid and insecure, then sticking to your decision to leave them now will be so much less painful in the long run – as another friend, Maria, learnt the hard way . . .

Maria, a bubbly and outgoing blonde, took a big risk when she fell for a gorgeous design student she met on holiday – especially as she left her boyfriend to be with him.

'Ben and I started to date when I got back to England, but in our second week together he went out, got drunk and slept with his ex-girlfriend, Katie.'

Although Maria wisely decided to cut her losses and run, Ben wasn't about to let her go. 'After weeks of him begging, sending letters and crying on my doorstep, I caved in and took him back,' she says. 'But then three weeks passed and I spotted Katie in a nightclub.

'Fortified by wine and the knowledge I looked HOT in my leather trousers, I felt confident when she walked over. But then she immediately burst out with "Maria, I'm soooo sorry that all this happened. The first time we slept together I felt so bad, and I told Ben we shouldn't do this to you, but the second time it was not my fault either, but I feel reeeeally bad."

'The second time!! I am a good actress and have a face of steel when needs be, so I smiled (I think I even patted her shoulder) and said, "That's OK" and walked away as though I already knew everything.'

Justifiably apoplectic with rage, Maria immediately found Ben and slapped him across the chops. This is when she says she definitely should have ended it. But terribly hurt and swiftly losing her resolve, she was unable to find the strength to break it off.

She explains: 'This time he said (and I believed him?) that he had been paralytic and half asleep when Katie got on top of him. Apparently, he'd thought she was me. Hmmm? But being young and insecure, after more wailing and gnashing of teeth, I took him back again.'

Crazy in love, Maria vowed to start anew and tried to push the betrayal from her mind. 'I also slept with my ex three times to even the score (dysfunctional? – oh yes). Alas, dear readers, the tale gets worse. As Maria and Ben's romance trundled on, one young lady always seemed to be lurking – another pesky former girlfriend called Emma.

'Every time we argued, Emma would offer Ben a shoulder to cry on,' Maria recalls. 'Then one night we went out, got drunk and I was sure I saw Ben's hand resting on her bum. I went ballistic, but he told me I was going mad. Which was clever, as at this point I had no belief in myself whatsoever.'

Like any good masochist, after a trial separation Maria took Ben back yet again, but finally, fearing total insanity, jetted off to Africa to work in an orphanage in Malawi.

'I was meant to be there for just a month to give myself some perspective but I ended up staying longer,' she says. 'The first couple of days Ben emailed and was clearly missing me, but then I heard nothing for a week. After a while I received an email from a friend saying she thought I should know that Ben was now seeing Emma. It seemed he couldn't be bothered to tell me it was over himself.' Maria and Ben had been together for two years and to this day have not spoken. He didn't tell her it was over, didn't say sorry or offer an explanation.

'That was just it,' Maria rants. 'It was as though he'd died. Then four years on I wrote him a letter to say that it was OK. It didn't hurt any more and if he wasn't going to give me closure, then I would take it for myself. I said good luck to him and Emma (who are still together, so maybe she's his soulmate) and told him that I too was happy.'

Although Maria admits that trust came hard after that, she did learn to have faith again. 'Without a doubt, it was falling in love with my next boyfriend and trusting him that healed me,' she explains. 'I also now know that my mother's advice, "If they do it once, they'll do it again," rings true. The only difference between the girl I just described and the person I am now, is my self-esteem.

'Over the years I wondered whether had I been stronger, would Ben have got away with it or even tried? I certainly wasn't the woman at the end that he met at the beginning. But I also know the fault lies with him. He was the one who chose to cheat – my only mistake was sticking around to let him hurt me again.'

When your self-esteem has taken a pounding over a prolonged period of time, it can be very hard to walk away unscathed.

Another friend recently confided that she was struggling to come to terms with her relationship ending, even though her partner had treated her very badly over a long, drawn-out space of time.

'Sometimes I feel like I deserved it,' she admits. 'The way I see it, I must have done something wrong. Why is he still getting under my skin?'

Anyone who claims that a relationship ended because it was one hundred per cent the other person's fault is deluded, but trying to take on all the burden of the blame can be equally self-destructive.

Instead, you have to accept that sometimes things just don't work out for a variety of reasons – other people's actions can be selfish and have a fundamental effect on us. At the same time, no one gets through life without making mistakes and misjudging situations.

In hindsight, we could all have done things differently, but without your own personal Tardis to travel back in time, it's impossible to know if the eventual outcome would have differed or not.

While you shouldn't bulldoze your way through life assuming that you always get it right, equally chewing the cud for all eternity just leaves you in a kind of no man's land, completely stuck and unable to move on. It's much better to accept that we are all fallible, but we have a right to expect to be treated well too.

Unfortunately, some people treat their partners with disrespect and cruelty, then dump the blame on them as a final brutal booby prize. But eventually you need to find acceptance that your relationship happened, you dealt with it to the best of your ability, it didn't work out, and now it's what happens in the future that counts.

So leave the self-doubt and blame behind, and draw a line under the past. And don't assume that lightning will strike twice either; it's never too late to start again afresh and make the most of new beginnings.

Which is something Janet discovered after going through a terrible time with her discourteous ex . . .

Successful career girl Janet had initially counted herself very lucky when she netted a handsome chap. Unfortunately, he also turned out to be a complete user, perfectly happy to exploit her kind and generous nature.

'Todd was supposed to be an actor, but I soon discovered he was a lazy git.'

While Janet was slaving away getting up at 5.30 a.m. to keep a roof over their heads and food on the table, Todd seemed perfectly content to do the bare minimum.

'The crunch came when – love being blind and all that – I saved up enough cash to book a lovely romantic break in

Spain for a week,' reveals Janet.

'I whisked us off, paying for the flights, the hire car and so on. While unpacking, I suggested we went for dinner in the local restaurant – nothing flash, just tapas and a bottle of cheap local plonk. Todd then announced that he hadn't brought any money, not a single euro. The cheeky bastard expected me to fund him and feed him all the way through the holiday as well as paying for the entire trip!'

Livid with her man, Janet carried on unpacking in silence, but while rummaging in her suitcase, she pulled out a strange plastic bag which definitely didn't belong to her.

'I opened it to find a huge wedge of dope, worth over a hundred and fifty pounds!' she reveals. 'So the bastard had no money to take me for dinner to say thanks for the holiday, but had plenty to fund his drug habit – and to add insult to injury, he smuggled the gear in *my* case!'

At that moment Janet had what can only be described as a flash of clarity – and fell straight out of love.

'I walked out of the apartment to an Internet cafe, booked a flight home, made him drive me back to the airport and left him on his own in Spain,' she says. 'I was really cut up by the way he'd treated me and sobbed all the way home on the plane, but I also knew the time had come for me to be assertive and move on.

'By the time he came back a week later I'd cleared our flat and moved out.'

In a textbook happy ending, six weeks later Janet met her future husband totally out of the blue. She has now been married for three years and has a little boy.

Well, Janet got her happy ending – and so can you. You just need to get over the next few hurdles of Broken Heart Boot Camp.

4.

The road to recovery and revenge

So what next?

You've washed, got dressed, stepped out of the house, bought some decent food, seen your friends and read up on other people's heartbreak.

But that doesn't mean you're not allowed the occasional relapse.

You probably still miss him from time to time, and thinking about your time together makes you sad. Plus everywhere you turn there are raw reminders that the life you had together has gone. There's that moment when you find a forlorn novelty toothbrush that Santa (i.e. you) bought him for Christmas, hiding behind a box of cotton buds in your bathroom cupboard. Suddenly, seeing a repeat of a *Top Gear* show you watched together feels like you've been stabbed in the heart, and you've noticed your bedroom doesn't smell musty in the morning any more.

Seeing Fearne Cotton on telly makes you throw your remote across the room with anger. So young, so successful, so fancied by your ex-bloke (unlike you). Then there is that half-eaten tub of Marmite taunting you in the cupboard. You hate it but can't bear to throw it away. In fact, everywhere you turn there are photos, keys to his flat, old sweatshirts and socks you borrowed, action DVDs that you'll never watch, and screwdrivers and DIY equipment which are as foreign to you as an eyelash curler is to the entire male population.

But, worst of all, are the love tokens. Birthday and Valentine's cards, and old handwritten notes stuck on the fridge or tucked in household drawers with poignant messages, such as 'love you', 'be back in ten' and 'your mother rang AGAIN.'

With all these reminders of him lying around, it's really no wonder you can't get him out of your head. So now it's time to deal with that painful paraphernalia – pronto. First, you need to sort it into two piles: stuff to be returned to him and stuff to be binned (or at least hidden away in a cupboard or attic).

But be careful – once again you're being cruel to be kind to yourself, and with a hornet's nest of emotions stirred up, you could find yourself wallowing and wondering 'what if' all over again. Don't, whatever you do, let too much thinking be toxic to your recovery . . .

Battling your inner masochist – phase two

1. He told me to stick his stuff in the post but I want to drop it off personally.

2. I've booked an appointment for a severe new haircut – just like Gwyneth Paltrow in *Sliding Doors*.

3. I am planning to get drunk and sleep with someone inappropriate.

4. I am about to accept a date with a boy I've never fancied. Well, at least someone wants to date me.

5. I will sleep with a boy I've never fancied. Well, at least someone wants to shag me.

6. When my ex calls at 1.30 a.m. and asks if he can come round 'for coffee', it would be rude to refuse.

7. I will lend him money, do his washing and drive him to his dinner date. At least he still needs me.

Right, let's address the list again. So you've bagged up all his stuff. Well done. But, eek, what's this? Rather than spring-cleaning your way to fresh beginnings, you are secretly plotting to get him back? When he sees that I've taken control and am getting on with my life, he'll realise what he's lost, you tell yourself.

So you book a wax, buy a new dress from Topshop, hand-wash your best undies, swamp yourself in the perfume he always liked, and gather up his stuff. Then you set off to his place, your heart brimming with nervous excitement and optimism – all overriding the little nagging doubt that is telling you: 'Sorry, do you not think this might seem a teeny-weeny bit *desperate*?'

So what happens when you arrive on his doorstep? As he opens the door, he looks at you surprised as, tellingly, you didn't call to warn him in case he told you not to come. Crafty. So you offer him the bags of his things with what you hope is a carefree smile.

'I thought you were going to post them?' he asks you coldly.

'Well, I was just in the area,' you stammer, wondering why he hasn't noticed your nice new dress.

'Thanks,' he replies, grabbing the bags from you while avoiding all body contact. You stand frozen to the spot, still straining with your carefree smile and waiting to be embraced or invited in at the very least.

'Well,' he says, taking a step backwards and looking at you like you're a bit odd. 'Er, see you then.'

Then the door is shut. In your face.

You go back to the car and speedily drive off. Your cheeks are streaming with tears before you even reach the end of his road. You are beside yourself.

Well, it could be worse – the door could have been answered by a half-naked girl or Fearne Cotton or your sister. But it could also have been a lot better. If you'd just posted his belongings, or handed them over to a mutual friend, you wouldn't now have to endure feeling rejected – *all over again*.

Please, for your own sanity, let this be the last time it happens. You see, once you've removed the objects making you sad, it's a chance for you to do something to cheer yourself up. Reclaim your living space as an environment that's all about you – your happiness, your independence, your stuff. Redecorate, buy fresh flowers, fill your frames with pictures of you and your girl pals, splash out on a

Nintendo Wii and invite your friends round for Cosmopolitans and virtual bowling. Soon, you'll remember that you don't need a man in your life to be happy and have fun. Single life does indeed rock.

Right, so let's talk about that radical new haircut you saw Agyness Deyn sporting in *Grazia*. While there are fashionistas out there who can seemingly pull off any bonkers barnet they like – and still look fabulous – in truth, the rest of us just don't have that luxury.

Take Alexa Chung, for example, she *does* have model looks, yet even she has fallen foul to the fickle hand of hairdressing fate and walked away with a dodgy hairdo she completely despises. As the lady herself says, 'It was probably a bad idea to make an important decision with a hangover, and hair-related decisions are as important as decisions can get.'

When you feel miserable and rejected, it is tempting to give yourself an image overhaul, but cut or dye your tresses with caution. I'm aware I'm sounding like your mother again, but if you really want a drastic new look, then why not build up to it gradually rather than going peroxide blonde in a day? It's a much, much safer option, believe me.

I once made the mistake of having a massive fight with my boyfriend before storming off to get my hair cut. In a fit of rage, I asked the hairdresser to hack my shoulder-length hair (which my boyfriend loved) into a short, trendy crop. *What on earth was I thinking?*

Er, I was thinking: 'This'll teach him', "I'm going to look sooo hot' and 'He'll curse the day he crossed me and I transformed myself into a goddess with men everywhere throwing themselves at my feet. Ha!'

But when I came back to face him, looking like Peter Pan's ugly, sideburn-sporting sister, I actually felt silly and humiliated. The thing is, it's bad enough being broken-hearted. So why torture yourself with shit hair too?

So what's next? Ah, getting drunk and sleeping with the man you met in the kebab shop or letting your slimy next-door neighbour feel you up. Yes, you were feeling lonely, but as one girl in the know confides: 'You tell yourself you're getting out there again, but afterwards you end up feeling suicidal and more alone and mismatched than ever.'

A lovely friend, Rebecca, also confides that trying to forget her ex by getting roaring drunk at a party and heading home with her flatmate's cousin was not the wisest decision she ever made.

'It really was a case of me shagging the first guy who paid me attention,' she admits. 'It was far from amazing. My heart wasn't in it, but half a bottle of tequila was. Halfway through I drifted off, and then when I woke up again, *still* having sex, I was not feeling enthusiastic. So once he'd finished, I got up, got dressed and left. After the 3 a.m. exit manoeuvre, cue self-loathing and sobbing in the shower the next morning. Not exactly the quick-fix I was looking for.'

You see, going on a date with or sleeping with that well-meaning, if slightly odd-looking, man, who just doesn't do it for you, is pretty much a kamikaze mission. He may seem kind, he may like you, he may agree with every damn thing you say. But, if the spark's not there, it's just not there. You can pour two bottles of Pinot Grigio down your neck, close your eyes and hope for the best. But you're still going to wake up, full of regret and repulsion, because you just shagged the toothless wonder from down the pub.

OK, maybe you decided against bedding a man with no teeth, but you could be contemplating sleeping with a man with no heart – YOUR EX – who, knowing that you are still weak and vulnerable, has called you or turned up at 2 a.m. looking for some loving.

The thing about blokes is they can be very good at separating love and sex. If they are drunk and horny, they know it is all too easy to hook up with a previously spurned ex-girlfriend. If you're still holding a light for him, then it might seem like a tempting opportunity to get the two of you back together – but that's not what he's thinking. A booty call at an obscene hour of the night adds up to only one outcome on his part – a bit of wham-bam-thank you-ma'am.

If he's particularly unscrupulous, then he might even give you the impression that he *wants* to get back together. But tread carefully, ninety-nine point nine times out of a hundred this will only be about sex. With his libido raging, he knows exactly what you need to hear in order to get you to drop your knickers. And if you can't accept that, then you are going to end up feeling broken and used.

As Theresa reveals, 'I had broken up with my ex (his choice) for about a month and was just beginning to come to terms with it all when he called out the blue. It was fairly late on a Saturday night and I was surprised when he asked me to come straight round to his "to talk". Stupidly, I did as he asked, but almost the minute I stepped in the house, he threw me on the bed, ripped off my dress and we had very heated, passionate sex. It totally took my breath away, but afterwards he just got straight out of bed, put on his clothes and went downstairs.

'I waited for a while, but when he didn't come back upstairs, I got dressed too and headed down to find him. He was in the lounge, watching the telly with a beer, and didn't even look up. Nervously, I sat down next to him and decided to get straight to the point, asking if this meant we were getting back together. But he looked me straight in the eye and said, "I'm sorry, Theresa, but nothing's changed."'

Devastated, Theresa left immediately and cried on and off for pretty much the next twenty-four hours. 'I just felt so used and ashamed of myself,' she says. 'I've never felt so cheap in my life and it really set me back after all the good progress I'd been making.'

Although, unlike Theresa, Holly knew exactly what was going on when her ex invited himself round in the wee small hours, that didn't necessarily make it any easier. 'Halfway through, I started crying,' she admits. 'The fact he was back for one night only made the experience so soulless, and I couldn't handle it.'

The thing about sex with your ex is that he is *still* your ex and a booty call does not mean an imminent return to a meaningful relationship. He might have moved on and be capable of no strings attached; you might kid yourself that you are too, but women attach a lot of emotions to sex. Being so intimate with someone you cared for is likely to stir up a lot of feelings – nostalgia, feelings of love, and sadness at what you've lost – all capable of setting you back dramatically in the recovery process.

Which is why Fay thought very carefully when allowing her former squeeze back to hers after a work do. 'He'd called it off a few weeks earlier, which I'd been upset about,' she says. 'But we still worked together so I had been very clinical about my feelings, not allowing them into the office with me. When he started getting a bit touchy-feely during an evening entertaining clients, I decided that I was quite up for it. But I also told myself that it would be no-strings sex and I couldn't allow emotions to come into it. So I decided that it would be about me using him and that I'd make it an empowering encounter.

'When we got back to mine, I skipped the formalities and guided him round various parts of my flat for mind-blowing sex, telling him exactly what I wanted. Afterwards, I went straight to bed and passed out. He stayed over, but the next morning I leapt out of bed, without any cuddles, kisses or soppy looks, and got ready for work.

'And do you know what? I wasn't faking it. I knew the relationship was over, so I just made the most of having one last hedonistic night. After that, he often hinted about it happening again, but I never went back. I left the relationship behind feeling it had ended with me holding the power.'

Booty call bounders

'When I fell asleep on my ex's sofa after a night out, he picked me up, put me in his bed, then tried to have his wicked way! That's one way of keeping your bed notches low, I suppose.'

'Every six months, my ex would get cold feet and tell me he needed "more space". I'd then spend a weekend crying in bed. Then he'd phone, tell me he loved me (the only times he ever told me) and we'd be back on. One time, the phone call included an invitation to go away for the weekend. I did. Immediately after sex, he said, "So we'll just go back to having a break?"'

'One guy I was seeing actually dared to say to me, "I don't think we're right for each other but can we be fuck buddies?" Nice! This is a man who would only see me when I went to his place – a good forty-minute drive from mine. It's not like he was offering plush hotel trysts with no strings!'

'I'd been seeing this guy for about three months when he went cold on me. He stopped getting in contact and told me he wasn't sure what he wanted. I said fine, and figured that was the end of that. Then one night he texted me at midnight asking if I wanted "some company". I said it would be nice to catch up but he should call me the following day when he was sober. Guess what? I didn't hear from him.'

Of course, it might not be about carnal desires. Maybe your ex just wants to exploit your good nature and willingness to help him out in all aspects of his life? Be wary of the man who is still tapping you for money, asking you to do his washing, or requesting a lift to his dinner date months after he canned you – as he just might be TAKING ADVANTAGE, as Dawn discovered . . .

'I lent my ex-boyfriend of five years eight hundred pounds because he was skint,' she says. 'We split up amicably, so I didn't think anything of it. I just thought he'd pay me back. However, a year later, when I asked if he could start giving me fifty pounds a month, he just shrugged and said, "Yeah, yeah, I'll sort it." Then he started seeing an Aussie barmaid, who dumped him on his birthday. He called me up to see if I wanted to go to Portugal with him on holiday – as he'd paid for them both! I agreed to go, although I was slightly miffed that he still owed me money and had been forking out on holidays for his bint instead.'

As it happened, holidaying with her lovelorn ex turned out to be a fairly unpleasant experience for Dawn. 'I spent the whole week counselling him, and he spent the whole time in a mood and disappearing to talk to her on the phone. When we got back, I had completely lost patience with him and emailed to ask, "Look, can you start paying me back, please?"

'Conveniently, for two months he didn't reply to one single email until, finally, I emailed his dad, saying, "Sorry to get you involved, but I really need my money back." I was just about to move to Germany and I did need it. Ten minutes later, I got an angry phone call from him, screaming how dare I contact his dad, but what else could he expect from "a selfish, two-faced bitch" like me! He said he'd contacted the bank for a loan, and he'd repay my money and hoped he would never have anything to do with me again.

'I wrote an abusive email, thought better of it, and replied with two words: "Thank you." So it took me two years and an abrupt end to our "friendship" to get my money back.'

Like Dawn, Nikki grew tired of her ex-boyfriend treating her as a convenience. 'We lived in the same area, but I only heard from him when he wanted something,' she reveals. 'He'd borrow money from me or get me to run errands for him but it was always a one-way street.

'The final straw came when he turned up at my door asking if I could drive him and his belongings to his new place, which was fifteen minutes down the road. He knew full well that I kept my car at my parents' place, a forty-five-minute commute away. So I said, "You expect me to go by public transport to pick up the car, drive back, take your belongings to your new place, then drive back to my parents to drop off the car, and get public transport back home again?"

' "Yeah," he said.

' "Er, fuck off," I said. "If you were a friend and contacted me just to see how I was, instead of when you needed something, then maybe!" '

Our next young lady, Jane, learnt the hard way that holding out for her ex was a waste of her valuable time and effort.

'I always thought I'd get back with my ex, Richard, but then he moved to London and said he wanted to play the field. We stayed friends, had dinner occasionally, but then he started seeing Serena, his first serious relationship since me, and my double: short, blonde, loud. Unsurprisingly, I found it difficult to see them together as I was still pining for him, but I kept up the friendship in the hope we might eventually get back together.'

Lo and behold, two years into his relationship with Serena, Richard called Jane to say he had broken up with her.

'When he asked if I wanted to meet up, I was thrilled,' says Jane. 'Maybe now he was planning to declare his undying love for me? But imagine my dismay when he asked if I could email Serena to see if she was all right! He explained that because I had been through a break-up with him, I'd be able to help her out. Charming!'

The trouble with 'being friends' with your ex is that feelings usually get in the way. Proper friendships depend on people being honest with each other, and if one person is secretly still in love, then all sorts of problems can arise – not least when someone new comes on the scene.

No matter how amicably you broke up, it's always good

to put some time and distance between you, as going from lovers to friends overnight takes some getting used to. And if you can't get over them while you continue to see them, sometimes it's just better to give up the ghost for good.

So you've decided he was a loser, a scoundrel and undeserving of your love. You've cut him out of your life, you're getting on with things and avoiding self-destructive behaviour. You've pretty much got your mojo back. But, in the spirit of guarding against all eventualities – what happens when, like a bolt out of the blue, you see him and suddenly all hell breaks loose?

I don't know what it is about me, but I have always attracted calamity. It's my default setting. I am the girl who tries to be cool, then trips, who breaks the heel of her shoe or accidentally tucks the back of her skirt into her knickers. I've come to realise that my destiny is always to be bumbling, and that is why, without fail, I will bump into exes or boys who cruelly rebuffed me at the worst possible moment.

When Jake, my college crush, canned me, it took all my strength not to sob into the Stilton I handled during my Saturday job on the deli counter at Sainsbury's. The knowledge he was already head-over-heels with another girl was humiliating enough – so why did fate then conspire for him to pop into the supermarket with his new lady in tow?

That morning, I'd overslept, so had driven straight to work without applying any make-up. And, as always, I was wearing a fetching navy blue tabard and the ugliest cap-hairnet hybrid known to man.

That Saturday, to my horror, I spied Jake and his glamour girl (damn it, she was very pretty indeed) at fifty paces, dawdling in the frozen goods aisle. Unfortunately, hiding was just not an option as I was in the midst of straining to hack through a piece of Parmesan cheese (surprisingly difficult). So, eyes down, I tried my best to cower under my fetching headwear and hope for the best.

But no such luck. Jake and his lady friend had clearly spotted me. As they passed, they both smiled (not unkindly). Mortified, I carried on wrestling with the Parmesan cheese, my heart rapidly sinking to the bottom of my sensible brown deli counter shoes. Finally, I finished serving my customer, made my excuses and headed off for ten minutes of stifled sobbing in the staff bogs.

My next mortifying encounter came courtesy of Ed, a guy who'd dumped me two weeks previously and who, to my horror, was seated across the room from me with a gaggle of girl pals in my local curry house. Unfortunately, this unexpected encounter came the day I'd chosen to leave the house in a T-shirt emblazoned with the word 'kinky' (I never learn). Like a true gentleman, he'd obviously pointed me out (a fact clarified by the staring and sniggers I then endured from his harem). Again, the humiliation hit me like a hammer, and that night I cried myself to sleep.

But, by far my worst ill-timed ex encounter involved a lad called Luke, who worked in the office above me. In truth, he didn't really qualify as an ex, as we had snogged only once at a work party. I already really liked him, so was chuffed when he agreed to meet me the following day.

In retrospect, I was a bit full on and too keen. Afterwards, I should have taken the hint, but instead I was a bit overzealous with my emails and texts, ensuring that he ended up ignoring me. He then snubbed me in the pub where everyone went on a Friday night, and because I was drunk, I cried in front of him – and all his workmates.

To this day, I have no idea why I reacted so badly to it all. I think it was knowing that we had mutual friends that really killed me. I couldn't bare the humiliation that he might be telling everyone that I was a freak (even though I was acting like one).

After that, I steered clear of the pub for a while and tried my best to avoid him. Some months later (by which time I was dating a lovely new beau), I was on the Northern Line tube commuting to work when I got thrown off at Camden Town. The date was 7 July and it turned out that London had been targeted in a terrorist attack. Three tube lines and a bus had been bombed.

A worrier at the best of times, I suddenly became very nervous about taking public transport. So I started to get the underground part of the way to work and walk the rest. Some days, I'd even walk all the way from my home in Golders Green to central London, more than six miles door-to-door.

The thing is, I wasn't very bright. Although I'd sometimes wear trainers, more often than not, I wouldn't bother. Instead, I'd pound the pavement in my girly pumps, not even contemplating that they were giving my feet zero support.

It was one such day that I rounded a corner to walk down a small deserted street near the office. As fate would have it, Luke was approaching at precisely the same moment. He saw me, I saw him. We were on the same bit of pavement, heading in the same direction. It seemed ridiculous to ignore him.

So I politely said hello and asked how his job was going. It was a bit awkward but he was being civil and I felt relieved that finally the ice had been broken. Then, just as I was on the verge of redeeming myself and proving to Luke that I was *not* a freak, I felt a weird 'pop' in my right foot. It was followed by a searing pain.

I stumbled slightly and panic surged through me – but not about my sudden injury. Luke already thought I was odd; how could I now announce that something had 'popped' in my foot? He'd think I was a complete fantasist. So, instead, I took the decision to carry on as if nothing had happened. I continued to chat inanely about work and forced myself to walk on, trying to look natural. To my horror, I realised that I was suddenly limping – like that wouldn't look odd at all?

If Luke noticed, he didn't let on; in all honesty, he was probably quite frightened. After five excruciating minutes, we finally arrived at the office and went our separate ways. Now safe from any further mortification, I burst into tears in front of my alarmed boss, who promptly packed me off to hospital.

Later, at St Bartholomew's Minor Injuries Unit, it transpired that all my manic walking in stupid shoes had led to a stress fracture and I now had a broken bone in my foot. Crutches and the geekiest cushioned trainers you'd ever seen were prescribed. And my status as Calamity Charlotte was thus restored.

* * *

So there you have it. I challenge you to beat that. Thankfully, I am not the only girl in the world who has endured a toe-curling encounter with an ex. You have to pity the poor lass who bumped into her children-hating ex with his now heavily pregnant new girlfriend. That really hurt.

Likewise, poor Gilly who, after a devastating break-up, decided to keep herself busy by taking a second job in a posh restaurant and bar.

'My job was greeting clients and helping with events, but one night, because it was so busy, I said I'd help with the coats,' she recalls. 'I was at the cloakroom entrance, when who do I see purposefully striding towards me? My disgusting ex with his gorgeous new girlfriend.

'Luckily, I was looking skinny that day and in a nice dress (one point to me). But he was practically giddy with the knowledge that he was embarrassing me, and said things like, "Wow, I didn't know things were so bad that you had to work here," and other patronizing comments. It was dreadful, and I burst into tears (a hundred points to him).'

Well, there is certainly one thing we can ascertain from this story – Gilly is definitely better off without her vitriolic ex. And while he may have momentarily felt smug at his small one-upmanship, he also shot himself in the foot. What girlfriend would be impressed by such a cruel display? And if she was, well, they're clearly made for each other.

When your ex has moved on before you, it can be quite a blow and it's easy to act emotionally and do something that you later might regret. When I broke up (amicably) with a long-term boyfriend, Adam, the hardest point for me came when, just weeks later, he announced he was off to Paris with a mystery young lady.

Strangely enough, I didn't take the fact that he was whisking a girl he'd known barely five minutes off to the ultimate city of romance very well. Particularly as he'd never suggested we go in our entire three years together. To add insult to injury, he'd conveniently decided to bugger off on this wonderful mini-break the same weekend I'd arranged to return to the home we'd shared to pick up my final belongings.

That Friday night, as I sorrowfully made my way across London (all the while imagining Adam and his new lady toasting each other with champagne on the Eurostar), I found to my dismay that the two tube lines I intended to use were down. By the time I let myself into our former love nest, I'd been travelling for well over two hours.

Tired and despondent, I bagged up my stuff as quickly as I could and began my long trek home to the opposite side of London. It was then I did something silly. En route I texted one of Adam's friends (his best-looking friend, in fact) to see if he fancied 'meeting up for a drink'. Well, if Adam was in Paris romancing a girl, then I had every right to go out and flirt with his friend, didn't I?

It seemed not. The lad in question graciously replied, saying thanks, but he was already out and about. I texted a few more times offering to join him, and although each time his reply was polite, he clearly wasn't taking the bait. And that was the end of that.

That is, until a few months later I saw Adam and he told

me gently that he knew about my texts. Apparently the friend had felt very uncomfortable about it. Not only Adam, but their entire circle of pals heard about it too. Suddenly, as I imagined them all discussing it, I felt extremely ashamed of myself. I told Adam tearfully that I'd acted without thinking when I'd been at my lowest – feeling sad, having just moved the rest of my stuff out, and devastated that he was in Paris with another girl.

He told me to forget it, that he understood, but I still wished I hadn't done it. The truth is that within minutes of sending those texts, I regretted it and realised I should have just called my best friend instead. She would have immediately talked me out of such impulsive behaviour, demanded I meet her to drown my sorrows, confiscated my phone and handed me pink wine instead – thus ensuring my dignity remained intact. But you live and learn.

What's worse? Seeing your ex with a model or a minger?

'My ex is now dating a beautiful plus-size model. When I heard he was seeing someone else, all it took was one scoot on Facebook (Devilbook!) to see this stunner who resembled Elle Macpherson. In the end, I had to delete him on Facebook because I couldn't sit and watch his relationship unfold before my eyes.'

'My ex's new girl is annoyingly perfect and gorgeous and, on the couple of occasions when I met her, actually really sweet. She's got an amazing figure, blonde hair and big boobs, and drives a flash car for God's sake! I think there's a bit of me that feels like she's a million times better, but I'm sure that's natural.'

'My ex is dating a girl who is not very pretty and has steadily put on weight since they started going out. At first, I felt really rubbish, thinking, "Hang on, if she's prettier than me, I must look awful!" Then I thought, wait a minute, I'm skinnier than her, I'm far more loaded and she's stuck with my ex while I'm dating a much nicer, more gorgeous guy. After that I just felt good about the whole thing.'

'An ex who treated me terribly, when I was still young and stupid enough to put up with it, is now married to the world's biggest bitch. I'm delighted! She dresses like a frump, too. Serves him right. Ha!'

'I bumped into my ex with his new girlfriend while out shopping – thankfully, I was with another, very fit member of his rugby team! Touché!'

At this point you'll be pleased to know that seeing an ex with her new bloke grates for men every bit as much as the opposite scenario does for us.

Although, it's pretty obvious male pride plays a part and they are less likely to admit their feelings. As one man says, 'I've ended up leaving most of my exes, but seeing them with another guy does grate. I suppose it's a natural male-competitive reaction.'

'It can be a killer,' another added. 'Especially if you're single. All you do is focus on the flaws (of which there are many) of their new man. You wouldn't believe how much you can hate someone you don't even know.'

And a third smart-arse lied, 'No, the restraining orders against all the women I've left means they have to stay at least a hundred metres away from me at all times.'

So, with the full horror of dates revisited, it's time for some futile suggestions on how to get over a bad ex encounter.

Back when we were about twelve, my best friend Paula and I thought New Kids on the Block were the best-looking boys ever. Fact. We'd strut around our bedrooms trying to pull off 'attitude' dance moves to 'The Right Stuff' and gaze at our *Smash Hits* posters trying to decide who was the swooniest. We even spent hours seriously discussing ways we could meet them, marry them and live happily ever after.

Fast-forward about two decades and the news filtered through that NKOTB were reforming (*wow-wee!*) Cue new soft focus press shots of the boys all grown up (and scarily close to forty). On hearing this triumphant news, Paula sent me a text message. 'God, have you seen NKOTB!' it read. 'What were we thinking?!' Upon Googling them, I had to agree. Little Joey McIntyre appeared to have improved slightly with age, but there was absolutely nothing appealing about the other four.

Not only did it highlight our extremely bad twelve-year-old taste, it was also a classic example of how revisiting crushes several years on can be extremely satisfying. When you discover the John Mayer lookalike who broke your heart all those years ago is now sporting a look much more like John Major, then why wouldn't you be smug?

Obviously, it's impossible to fast forward ten years with the hunk who just wronged you. But surfing on Facebook to find your back-catalogue of heartbreakers just might inspire you. Among the motley crew there's bound to be a formerly svelte suitor who now looks like he's donned a fat suit. And what on earth happened to the hot rocker boy whose glossy long hair always drew comparisons to Anthony Kiedis? Yes, that's right, he's morphed into William Hague.

If that doesn't give you a boost, then there's nothing for it. It's time to get on Photoshop and scan in a picture of the wrong-un who left you in this sorry state. Add a few chins, go crazy with his receding hairline and crank up the pounds. Hell, it may be pathetic but sometimes such childish actions are just the tonic.

Dignity v Dastardly

So, it's the age-old question – when you've been treated despicably should you do the dignified thing of turning the other cheek or should you go the whole hog and extract a wicked revenge?

Any good self-help book (and my mum) will tell you not to do the bad stuff. Be dignified, they'll say, show them you're a stronger, bigger person; don't sink to their level. But sometimes it's just too tempting. Surely it must be time for some more show-and-tell therapy?

Let's begin with Milly who took a mild but effective revenge when her 'sweet' boyfriend turned out not to be quite the good sort she'd thought.

'To begin with Gerard was attentive and funny and always claimed he was crazy about me,' she says. 'But then there were times when he was quite unreliable and seemed more interested in hanging out with his mates. For a while I put up with it because he was so cute and endearing. But as time went on he got worse. He never stood me up but he'd half-make plans or we'd be out and about and suddenly he'd need to be somewhere else.'

Then, one day, Gerard's flaky behaviour fell into place. The news filtered through to Milly that a few of her boyfriend's 'mates' were actually of the female variety. What's more, they were more than just 'friends'.

'Livid, I immediately broke up with him and quickly learned he'd picked up with one of the girls he'd been two-timing me with,' she says.

But Milly was determined that Gerard would not escape scot-free. When a suitable opportunity arose on the magazine she worked for, Milly wrote up the tale of Gerard's betrayal. Determined to keep her dignity, she was honest, not vicious, but it gave her a chance to redress the balance and expose his two-timing without actually naming him or the girl.

'Revenge is sweet,' she says. 'We all worked in the same industry, so I knew word would quickly get around. Sure enough, it wasn't long before his girlfriend saw my article and read him the riot act.

'When I saw Gerard at a party a few weeks later he was spitting blood that I'd outed him in public. It was all very satisfying and hopefully taught him a valuable lesson.'

Milly went on to meet the man of her dreams and now has two little children – and all heartbreak over Gerard is long forgotten.

Phillippa, like any good psycho, wasn't content just to mope around and cry when her ex swiftly dispatched her and wheeled in her replacement. Instead, she took great delight in leaving a trail of destruction on Facebook, all designed to freak out her former love's new lady friend.

'It started with me joining various networks to try and see my ex's new girlfriend, but gradually got worse,' she admits. 'One night, my friends and I were drunk and did something really bad. After hacking into his Facebook page, we used his user name to comment on pictures of his new girlfriend, writing things like, "Not keen on that top, babe" and "You've looked better".

'Then I went through a list of his exes, either sending them messages via Facebook or writing on their wall. I hoped they'd write back and make his new girlfriend paranoid. They did and I heard that the new girlfriend was far from happy.'

While Phillippa's actions were not very nice, I don't think she ranks as the most evil genius out there. Compared to some, she's small fry.

So, without further ado, let's meet the ladies whose wrath knows no boundaries. The Mistresses of Vengeance who will stop at nothing to teach the men who dared to cross them a lesson they would never forget. Hell hath no fury like a woman scorned!

When Leigh discovered her boyfriend had been cheating on her with a work colleague she decided to get even – with his flat.

'I couldn't control the burning rage inside me as I came to terms with his betrayal,' she says. 'Four years of love down the pan.'

Consumed with anger, she began her campaign of terror by hurling a wine bottle at the wall – which, unfortunately, being a new-build apartment, didn't smash and left a gaping hole from the bedroom through to the lounge. Whoops.

Next, knowing that her chap was obsessed with grooming his hair, she snapped his beloved straightening irons in half. Then she trampled all over his precious CD collection in her scratchiest heels, and then pondered on what she could do next.

'I've always read about women slicing their cheating husband's shirts with scissors, so I thought I'd have a go at that too,' she says. 'As I neatly packed them back into their suit bags and cut his ties in half, I smirked with satisfaction.'

With her work now done, Leigh left triumphant, but with just one more parting gift up her sleeve – this time for her boyfriend's mistress.

'Knowing that he was off to his bint's birthday party the following Saturday (I knew because we were meant to be going together), I called the venue where it was being held and pretended to be her. I took great glee in cancelling all her catering plans, party and everything else. I'm not sure what happened to her party in the end, but I hope she liked her surprise.'

When Nadine was dumped by a waster and a scoundrel, she merely bided her time until the perfect opportunity for revenge arose.

'After Graham and I broke up, he moved in with some of my friends as they were desperate for a housemate,' she reveals. 'But after treating me badly, he was an arsehole to them too. He didn't pay the rent on time, didn't clean up and was pretty selfish.

'One night, I went to visit my friends with two bottles of wine. We drank one, opened the second and drank some of that, and then one of them joked about how funny it would be if we pissed in one and gave it to Graham.' One friend, Gary, immediately volunteered to do the deed and headed upstairs to the bathroom with the half-full bottle.

'It came back full and a bit warm, so we put it in the fridge for an hour. Then, when it was nice and chilled, I headed upstairs with it to Graham's room. After knocking, I walked in, smiling sweetly, and handed him the wee-wee wine.

'"I hate that there are bad vibes between all of us," I told him. "I just wanted to offer you a bottle of wine to say no hard feelings." Graham immediately replied, "Oh, thanks, Nadine! That's very considerate of you," and then took a massive gulp of the wine right in front of me. I had to use every ounce of willpower to keep a straight face.

'We then chatted for a few more minutes about how we should all be friends and he took another gulp or two of the special vintage. I then made my excuses and went back downstairs to my friends.

'To this day, he still doesn't know what happened and I still smile to myself every time I think of it!'

When Anna's clothes shop manager boyfriend announced he was going travelling for a year, not only did she selflessly refuse to stand in his way, but she spent the best part of two weeks scouring the shops for thoughtful 'going away' presents. Unfortunately, it seemed her chap was not quite the good egg she'd envisaged.

'At his going-away party I was horrified to overhear two women in the toilets discussing whether I had any idea he'd been sleeping around,' she says. 'Armed with this news, I decided to pick my moment, and said nothing for the rest of the evening, playing my part of the devoted girlfriend.'

The following day Anna's boyfriend asked if she'd mind transcribing his phone numbers from his mobile to his diary for the trip. In the middle of doing so, a timely text came through from a woman revealing that she'd seen him just a couple of nights before.

'I then read all of his texts,' says Anna, 'and discovered some very graphic messages from several women he was clearly sleeping with. Unable to bite my tongue any longer, I confronted him, saying that I had overheard rumours. To which he had the gall to claim that a lot of his female friends were jealous of our relationship and had done it out of spite. I didn't mention the texts and bid him off on his travels.

'Three days in, he sent a round robin email to his whole family, me, his pals and every other woman he'd slept with. He also emailed me a load of gushy crap separately about how much he missed me. Over the next six months, I carried on sending him emails, keeping them short and sweet, while I found out various incriminating pieces of evidence about him stealing from the shop and the like.

'Then, on his thirtieth birthday, I sent an email to him and every other person in his email address book, including his former bosses and his other lovers, telling him I knew what he'd done, about all the affairs, all the one-night-stands, and the thefts, and that I'd given all the evidence to the police and his employers.

'I also suggested that he might do well to have an STD check since that was how I had caught him (it wasn't, but it had the desired effect). I got word very quickly from Cambodia that all hell had broken loose and his birthday had been ruined. I did have to disband my email account, though.'

And the moral of this story? Don't mess with Anna.

The revenge chronicles

'I like Facebook rants – usually exposing an ex's lack of substance in the manhood area.'

'Pulling his best friend works a treat.'

'Best one I have heard is about a woman who rubbed dried chillies into her husband's boxers before he went out. He came back later in agony. It confirmed her suspicions, as her best friend was suffering too.'

'My friend is moving out of her boyfriend's place and in with her ex. He is going to go mental.'

'I heard of a lady who found out her husband was cheating so she used his toothbrush to clean the toilet. Not nice!'

'I still wish sometimes that I had thrown my ex's vinyl collection out of a top-floor window . . . he would never have recovered.'

'Superglue in any car, house or bike lock works a treat.'

'Become hugely successful and live a significantly more fun and eventful life.'

> 'One friend shaved her hair off in a drunken moment and posted half her hair to her ex and half to his mum. I haven't heard from her for years; I think she was actually quite disturbed.'

Indeed, revenge doesn't always pay, as Grace reveals.

'When a guy dumped me because he wasn't getting enough sex, I got revenge by going out with his best friend,' she says. 'What I didn't realise was that he'd never been in a relationship before and was a virgin. He became far too intense too quickly, so after six months I ended it, which completely broke his heart – but the ex didn't bat an eyelid! Not the best executed plan.'

One sensible lady points out, 'I would suggest that taking revenge doesn't ultimately make you feel better. It just makes you look bitter and reminds him why he left you in the first place.' It's also interesting to note that it seems to be more unusual for a man to take revenge – it really is a girl thing. As one man says, 'There's no point taking revenge, heartache is just part of growing up', and a second suggests his ex 'diminished herself' in her pursuit of vengeance.

And let's not forget that while the extreme settling of scores might seem justified from your perspective, the eyes of the law might see things differently. What happened to the woman who sent a letter to her cheating boyfriend's workplace claiming he had HIV and hepatitis and was keeping it from his workmates? That's right, she was taken to court and fined two hundred and eighty pounds.

Then there was the real-life *Fatal Attraction* case study who decided to break into her ex-boyfriend's home, slash all his clothes and, er, kill his pet cat. Strangely enough, her explanation that hurting her former lover was her 'coping mechanism' didn't leave the court particularly sympathetic. She was ordered to carry out one hundred and eighty hours of community service and pay nearly a thousand pounds in compensation, plus court costs.

So, unless you want Google searches on your name to reveal the title 'kitty killer' forever more, then you might want to try something a little more subtle.

5.

Moving on

So you've indulged the wicked thoughts, defaced his photo and perhaps even cut holes in the crotch of his favourite suit. (Sshh, it's OK, no need to tell.)

But now you've had your fun it really is about moving on. Remember bitterness in a lady is a very unattractive quality. While your friends, work colleagues and family will happily slate him for hurting you at first – if you're still harping on like a broken record six months later, then they will likely label you a break-up bore.

While you are still replaying his actions over and over in your head, trying to fathom how someone could treat you like that or fantasising that you had the world's most perfect romance that can never be replaced, you are stuck in a rut. The cold, hard truth is that your ex has most likely moved on already and probably isn't thinking about you at all. The only person holding you back from a full, happy recovery is you. Everyone is different, but subconsciously you probably already know what you need to do to take that final step.

As Sarah reveals: 'I was dumped about six weeks ago and I'm still unsure about why he broke up with me. Apparently, the spark had gone, but for ages I couldn't help thinking that it was something I'd done wrong. I tortured myself thinking if only I had done this or that better, or if circumstances had been different we'd still be together. But, gradually, I had to move on and come to terms with the fact that maybe he just didn't think I was The One.'

Sarah now says she has come to the slow realisation that maybe he wasn't the right one for her either. 'Having time to reflect on a relationship somehow makes it easier to deal with,' she says. 'It allows you to see the flaws, the compromises you made and the disappointments you chose to ignore. And it made me realise that even if we'd stayed together it never would have worked.

'I wanted more, not the big things like marriage, kids or commitment, but things that we all deserve from a relationship – such as closeness, communication and just to know that we're "that girl", the girl he thinks the world of, the one he can't believe he's found, and the one who, eventually, he can see spending the rest of his life with.'

We're used to having some kind of control over our destiny but when someone breaks up with you, or your seemingly perfect romance crumbles before your eyes, there is a period when you desperately search for some kind of reprieve or chance to make things better.

It is frightening to feel you are being swept away in a situation over which you have no control. But the way you can regain control is to see, as Sarah did, that you do have a choice. You can look to the future and move on by finding your own personal coping mechanism to lay all that bad feeling or hopeless nostalgia to rest.

How to move on – real tips from girls who've been there

'It's a little like the process you go through when someone dies. Allow yourself time to grieve and sob. Only when you have done that will you move on to feeling angry and ripping up photos.'

'When you split up you worry you'll never meet another man. But I had a whole year of dating every man who asked me out and I loved every minute of it. It helped to make me feel desirable again.'

'Delete all contact, change your phone number and block his emails. Don't stay friends, it's impossible, especially when he meets someone new. The men to women ratio means men always find a new partner first!'

'I wrote my ex a long letter telling him how let down I felt and how his reckless behaviour had left me completely distraught. I never sent the letter, but writing it was really cathartic.'

'Go out and get drunk, and then get on with your life.'

'When my boyfriend broke up with me, I forced myself to go to the gym every day. I soon found that pounding the treadmill and swimming really helped my stress levels and also gave me plenty of time to collect my thoughts. Not only did it help me to get over my heartache, I also ended up with a great bikini body to boot!'

So you're almost there, you just need to give yourself that final push. So while you're pondering over which method will work best for you, it's time for a quick blast of rehabilitation through the uplifting medium of music – oh yes!

As you know, moping melodies were officially banned in the immediate aftermath of Life Without Him. But now you are feeling stronger and more optimistic, it's time to get a playlist together of the following 'I'm moving on' songs to seal the deal in your mind.

And before you ask: no, we're not going to bawl drunkenly 'Didn't We Almost Have It All' by Whitney to the perpetrator of our heartbreak in a crowded karaoke bar. It may have been what my good friend Kate did, but the less said about that the better, for everyone's sake.

Music to bid boys goodbye

'Gold' – Beverley Knight

When I spoke to friends about their favourite, empowering, moving-on ditties, I had two slightly embarrassed recommendations for this song. But you've gotta love a bit of Bev. In this classy ballad she tells her ex (in a rather dignified fashion) just the way it is – that's he an ignorant fool who let a very precious entity (a.k.a. her) slip through his fingers. What a numpty.

'I'm Outta Love' – Anastacia

In this poignant anthem, husky diva Anastacia sums up that feeling when you've done everything you can to make a relationship work but ultimately lost patience because your chap just isn't prepared to put the work in. Through the medium of song Anastasia finally informs her man that it ain't a one-way street. In other words, 'Sorry, Sunny Jim, you took the piss, now I'm outta here.' I am reliably informed this is also a great karaoke track.

'Fighter' – Christina Aguilera

Raising the tempo again we have that small but forceful firecracker Christina Aguilera. With determined attitude she blares out a feisty, in-your-face message for the sadistic bully boyfriend who thought he'd broken her. 'No,' she exclaims. 'You're wrong. The fact you treated me mean made me stronger and wiser.' Yeah!

'You Oughta Know' – Alanis Morissette

Right, time to get angry. Ooh, can you feel the venom? This song first had me gasping in awe when, aged seventeen, I walked round college listening to *Jagged Little Pill* on my Walkman. And fourteen years on it still has the same impact. I love the way Alanis, like a truly deranged and spurned ex-girlfriend, flits from being quiet and composed to out-of-control pure venom. You can actually picture her crazed psycho smile as she gives her philandering ex what for. Grrr.

'I Hate You So Much Right Now' – Kelis

Again, the scary wrath of a wronged woman. In this ballsy 'don't mess' outpouring, Kelis dedicates her musical tale of a worthless, cheating boyfriend to all the girls out there who've also been lied to. She screams about how much she hates him and then warns that she's no fool and just might take revenge.

'Killing in the Name' – Rage Against the Machine

Not really a break-up song but, boy, does screaming 'motherfucker' at the top of your voice cleanse the soul. In fact, listening to Rage Against the Machine full stop is the perfect music remedy for when someone has treated you like shit and you want to get ANGRY. Put it on your iPod and knock the crap out of a punch bag down the gym. You'll feel so much better afterwards.

'King of Wishful Thinking' – Go West

Ah, calm. Now all the anger is gone, it's time for an upbeat eighties track to set you on your way. This song is all about facing up to your heartache, pulling yourself together and being optimistic. 'Hey, shit happens,' Peter Cox croons on this favourite from the *Pretty Woman* soundtrack. 'But that doesn't mean I'll always feel this way.' And quite right he is too.

'I Don't Need a Man' – Pussycat Dolls

While as a general rule I am loathe to take guidance from a bunch of slutty types who think it's accept-able to taunt men with statements like 'don't cha wish your girlfriend was hot like me', on this occasion the prick-teasing harem have got it right. An upbeat anthem about being self-sufficient and not needing a man to be happy. Bravo.

Single Ladies (Put a ring on it) – Beyoncé

A triumphant 'up yours' to the commitment phobe who refused to propose but now is green with jealousy that his former squeeze has moved on. The upbeat 'ho-ho-hos' really make this song and always give me a vision of sexy semi-clad ladies flexing their bare ring fingers in the faces of marriage-shirking exes – all the while pulling off some great Beyoncé booty moves. 'Uh-huh, you had it, but you lost it.'

'Wild Women Do' – Natalie Cole

Let's finish with another eighties classic from the *Pretty Woman* soundtrack – arguably *the* must-have album for any lady. This ballsy refrain is all about getting out there and enjoying yourself with hedonistic glory. 'Guess what, you don't have to conform or take second best,' Natalie says. 'It's actually all about YOU.' Hurrah – three cheers for Nats! A perfect ending to a great empowering playlist.

The thing about exes is there comes a time when you simply have to stop thinking about them. It doesn't matter who he's now dating, whether he regrets his actions or regularly boasts to his knuckle-headed mates that he's shagging half of Swindon every Friday night or has taken a vow of celibacy to become a monk.

The next few (and final) weeks of Broken Heart Boot Camp are all about YOU. It's time for you to step back out into polite society with a packed social diary that would put Paris Hilton to shame. By spending the next few weeks going out, spending time with friends and making things happen, you will realise that you don't need to be in a relationship to feel happy or fulfilled. And you might even score a nice snog too. Bonus!

A few weeks after I'd been through the mill with a particularly sad break-up, I decided to travel to Blackpool with seven female friends for my birthday. I'd figured that a weekend of cheap booze, bingo and kiss-me-quick hats was just what I needed to take that final step towards full recovery – and it did indeed prove to be the perfect tonic.

My friends and I checked into a cheap bed and breakfast near the North Pier for about fifteen pounds a night (including breakfast – bargain!) and spent our first day exploring the Pleasure Beach and Tower Ballroom. The sun was shining and it was glorious.

Then, after downing several fluorescent cocktails, we went on the Big One rollercoaster and scared ourselves silly. That night, we quaffed lukewarm sparkling wine and pizza in our B&B before hitting the town in fancy dress. I'd imposed a cowgirl theme on my friends (classy) and we stepped out in multi-coloured hats, brandishing water pistols. We were in Yates Wine Bar when my friend Claire, a cheeky Northern lass, and I both stopped to admire a rather dashing young man waiting to be served at the bar.

'Go on!' she said, elbowing me in the ribs.

So, doing as I was told, I promptly aimed and squirted my handsome target with my water pistol. I hit him right in the eye – oops. Startled, the young man jumped, rubbing his water-drenched eye, and scanned the room for the perpetrator. Of course, Claire and I quickly pretended to look the other way. But the fact we were doubled up, crying with laughter (and wearing cowboy hats) slightly gave us away.

Suddenly, I saw my victim had us in his sights and was pushing his way through the crowd towards us. Eek!

'Was that you?' he asked with a bemused expression on his face when he finally reached us. I noticed water was still dripping off his nose.

Like two naughty schoolgirls, we stood there silently, trying to suppress our smirks. Finally, Claire shook her head, as I nodded mine, all the while biting my lip.

'Why, you little buggers!' he replied, but there was definitely a smile developing on his face. Then we all burst out laughing.

It turned out my unwitting victim was called Jim and he'd travelled to Blackpool from Nottingham for a drunken weekend with his football team. As we chatted, I liked him a lot. Not only was he easy on the eye, he was extremely funny and nice – and he appeared to like me!

Well, that was it, for the rest of the night Jim tagged along with us and became an honorary cowgirl. As we toured from bar to pub, and eventually arrived at a club, our group continued to expand as various friends also met nice young men. Jim and I laughed and joked all night and it wasn't long before I got my birthday snog – hurrah!

Then, at about 3 a.m. we all staggered back to our hotel and demanded the night porter open the bar . . . and put some music on . . . and make us chip butties. The poor man was all things to all people as he dashed about tending to the deep-fat fryer, fetching us gin and tonics, and desperately pleading for us to keep the noise down.

By 6 a.m. everyone was flagging, so reluctantly I swapped numbers with Jim and bid him farewell. Then Claire and I staggered upstairs to our twin room to drink pints of water and dissect the evening's events. I just remember lying there feeling really cheery and elated. Not just because I was drunk or had met a nice boy, but because I knew that everything was going to be fine. I'd got through the worst of my break-up and out the other side. I was back having fun and loving every minute hanging out with my friends. Life after my ex did exist!

The following day, nursing sore heads, my friends and I headed off for a brunch and then made our different ways home. To my delight, Jim called me that week and we did actually meet up again, but it never really developed into anything. Given the distance between our homes and the fact I'd just broken up with my boyfriend, we decided we'd be better off being friends.

A wise decision as it happens. Not only did it give me some more valuable time and space to be single and do my own thing, but Jim and I are also good friends to this day.

So with a new determined focus on having fun the painful thoughts about your ex should start to fade. However, sometimes, as you get out there and attempt to forget him, you might be aware of an unwelcome figure lurking in the shadows. Even when you're ready to move on, you might have some difficulty in shaking off your ex.

Your former lover may continue to linger like a bad

smell. He doesn't want you but he's not prepared to let you go either. There may be little texts telling you he still misses you, sharing his worries about his day at work, or he might call for a 'chat' every other day. But don't be fooled, these are NOT signs he wants to get back together. He just can't let go. He doesn't want to be with you, he's just not sure how to be without you either.

As this isn't helpful for either of you, it needs to be nipped in the bud if you're going to have a chance of moving on. As long as he's hanging around, he'll be a constant reminder of your relationship, whether it's making you remember the good times as you look back with rosy specs or the awful way you felt at the end. It just leads to confusion all round.

Plus he could be jeopardising your chances with potential new suitors – something that Tanya almost let happen . . .

'When I first became involved with Gareth I should have really known better,' she says. 'I committed two cardinal dating sins – first, he was friends with my ex-boyfriend and secondly, he was the ex of one of my best mates, Cathy. All very incestuous.'

For two years, Tanya and Gareth had a pretty up and down relationship. 'It was long distance but in my mind we were exclusive – although with hindsight I think I was seeing what I wanted to see.

'Through the course of the relationship Gareth remained friends with Cathy, which I was fine with as I trusted her completely. Yet he constantly picked me up and put me down like a toy, whenever it suited him.'

The relationship really came to a head in the summer of 2007 when Tanya and Gareth jetted off on a holiday to Corfu together. 'Before we got on the plane I overheard Gareth making a very indiscreet and badly coded phone call to a mate, and I suspected he'd been shagging someone else the night before we flew out. I didn't have any proof, though, so just about endured the holiday by trying to make the most of it.'

But on their return, a mutual friend of Tanya and Cathy dropped a bombshell. 'She told me that just before Gareth had gone away with me he'd tried it on with Cathy during a night out. She'd rebuffed him, so he'd continued to drink himself into a stupor, eventually turning up at her front door in the middle of the night slurring and screaming in the street that he loved her.

'Armed with this little revelation, I sat Gareth down and a very calm discussion ensued. He denied it, of course, but then claimed that he hadn't seen us as "exclusive", and that if he had managed to seduce Cathy he wouldn't have done anything wrong!

'A few weeks later, as I pondered the future, Cathy and I went for a girlie spa break for a few days to have a proper think and a good stiff drinking session. The mini-break culminated in an almighty piss-up with the rest of my girlfriends and their partners. That night, I met Larry, who had tagged along with my friend's husband. We got on like a house on fire and ended up staying out until 6 a.m.

'Now, although I liked Larry, I was still hung up on Gareth, whom I'd been texting and calling for days without response. Larry had been texting me, though, saying how much fun he'd had the night before, and we exchanged some cheeky banter.

'It was a bank holiday weekend, so as I nursed my hangover later that Sunday evening, I had two texts arrive at more or less the same time. One was from Gareth, and read, "At a loose end tomorrow, wanna come to mine?" The other was from Larry, politely asking, "Would you let me take you out for dinner tomorrow night?"

'There was something about that moment – the timing of those messages was significant. I felt it was a chance for me to break the cycle. I was still torn, though, but thankfully my mum was there to help me decide with a few words of wisdom. She told me that Gareth had had his chance and now the nice new lad deserved his.

'She also suggested that I tell Gareth exactly why I couldn't meet him, because that's what he deserved. So that's what I did. I accepted the invitation from Larry and then texted Gareth, informing him I had a dinner date with a lovely guy I'd met through friends and that I'd speak to him another time.

'The vitriolic outburst that followed from Gareth was the single most satisfying thing I have ever experienced. Basically, it went along the lines of who the hell did I think I was, and fucking fine, I could fuck off and have a nice life . . . I realised the reason he was so angry was because I'd given him a taste of his own medicine, dropping him when it was convenient for me. He didn't like it one little bit.

'I was expecting to feel broken and sad and scared that I'd lost someone really important, but all I felt was a weight lifted off my shoulders. In fact, I felt so happy I couldn't stop smiling.

'It was the best thing I ever did. After our dinner, Larry and I were inseparable. Within a couple of months, we'd booked a three-week holiday to Thailand and we were talking long-term future. I've been with him almost two years now and I'm pretty sure he's The One.

'Eventually, I received an apology by email from Gareth saying he had just been "shocked by my honesty". He also apologised for not fighting harder for me and said that because I'd made a decision to move on, he'd decided I didn't need him "hanging round in the shadows".

'I assume he'd convinced himself he was doing me a favour, that clearly if he'd stayed in touch, I would have been powerless to resist his charms and start a new relationship. I'm sure he knows the truth deep down, though.

'There's nothing more empowering than ending a crappy relationship by giving a bloke like Gareth a taste of his own medicine. Not to mention finding something and someone a million times better!'

Ahh . . .

But while Tanya's story is heart-warming and she obviously struck gold with Larry, it also doesn't hurt to give yourself a bit of time and space before you consider getting serious with someone new. While puckering up with a nice chap here or there is going to give you a boost, it's probably best to avoid going straight into another intense relationship.

Rebound romances can often be clouded by the fact you haven't fully recovered from the last one you were in. If you're still drowning in a sea of resentment and hurt, diving head-first into another love affair could be dicey. Chances are you'll still be thinking about your ex a lot and will therefore use your new romance as a kind of buoyancy aid to get you over it. As Camilla's story illustrates . . .

'After my first boyfriend and "true love", I went head-first into a rebound relationship with Emilio from Spain, an older man with a sexy accent, who rescued me from the dump. Well, that's how I felt when I met him. However, when he announced to me that he was moving to England just as I was starting university, I knew in my heart of hearts it was a mistake.

'While he stayed in my home city I was a first-year student in London. I saw him at weekends and wrote him long love letters that really masked my heartache for my ex. I should have been starting a new life with new friends, but instead I made tearful phone calls to him from my room.

'However, my wake-up call came when he told my parents that he disapproved of my living in a house with other males. When asked what he would suggest, he said (in absolute seriousness) he would prefer it if I lived with nuns. He was staunchly Catholic, thirty-four, and deluded. I think I dumped him two days later. He told me I would never come to anything. I sometimes wish he could see how lovely my life is now.'

So, rather than grabbing the first mediocre lifeline you're offered, try to have fun and be on your own for a while – and get selfish!

This is a mantra the newly single Sarah says she has

come to realise. 'When you're in a relationship you make compromises and decisions because you're in love,' she says. 'Maybe things that you would never have even considered before. When you're single, you wouldn't dream of spending time with someone else's family on a summer's evening, when you could be in a pub beer garden with the girls. You no longer have to bother with pointless arguments, getting in a huff over who has to do the washing up, and conversations like "Where do you think this relationship is going?"

'For me, being single means anything is possible – travelling without thinking about his feelings, moving halfway across the country for a job, staying out all night without having to check in with him – basically, just being selfish, and doing what I want to do when I want to do it.'

She's right. If you can just get to a healthy place where you realise you don't need a man to survive and are capable of going it alone, your self-esteem will reap the rewards and you'll hit the ground running.

And, bizarrely enough, when you are feeling comfortable and content in your own skin, and not remotely bothered about meeting a man, you will subconsciously give off very attractive vibes. With this sexy new confidence radiating from every pore, it's likely that you'll soon be inundated with offers – but do you really want them?

You see, as Sarah points out, now is the perfect opportunity to do all those things you've talked about but never found time for. And I'm sure you'll also agree that up until recently, holding down your relationship was extremely time-consuming. Where did all those hours, days and years go? Highly likely they passed in a blur of nights in, filled with meaningful discussions about what Stacey Slater will do next on *EastEnders* and whether Vernon Kay is actually funny or not. Then there was the refusal to waste money on fun nights out and extravagances in favour of paying for that new DFS sofa.

Add that to hours of sulky silences after you cancelled 'nookie night' due to adverse body conditions – i.e. you were 'tired' or felt 'bloated' from eating a whole Domino's pizza. Throw in a few Sunday afternoons of penance spent entertaining your difficult in-laws. Hours spent slaving to make and then serve that tricky Nigella recipe, only for that infuriating member of his family to sit there with a face like a slapped arse and not even offer to help clear up.

Fact is, you'll NEVER get those hours back – but on the plus side, being single now means that things are looking up. Now your bedtime is no longer dictated by his 6 a.m. starts, and it turns out you can watch telly or read beyond 10 p.m.! Woo-hoo!

Gloriously, you can sit on the sofa and gabble loudly on the phone to your friend for hours on end without him banishing you to the bedroom because your constant 'jibber jabba' is interrupting *Ross Kemp on Gangs*. The bathroom will once again be reclaimed as a place of peaceful sanctuary without him banging on the door during your relaxing bubble bath to kindly inform you that he's now 'touching cloth' and can you 'get a bloody move on?' And let's not forget the arguing. Thank goodness you'll never have to spend another second having those awkward, strained discussions about how you can improve or mend your relationship.

Suddenly, your weekends and evenings are freed up – and if you make the most of it, you'll find that being single is actually a lot more fun than being shacked up. You'll soon find that the friends you saw only once every couple of months will start to make more of an effort now that you are too. Finding yourself single and lonely can be daunting, but if you show you're willing, any good friend will be there to help you through the break-up, no matter how lacklustre your friendship had become while you were happily coupled-up.

But you don't have to rely on other people to make you happy again. Indeed, with no man to worry about, now is the time for your very own *Jim'll Fix It* adventures to begin. Without further ado, start by writing a list of all the achievable things you'd like to do but never got round to. Compose your wish list and then email it to all your girlfriends to see who wants to join you.

Plan girls' nights out where you dress up in posh frocks, drink cocktails all night and dance to the wee small hours. And book weekends away – mini-breaks to country cottages, days by the seaside or city breaks to lovely places abroad.

When I went through my last break-up, I did something I'd not done for years – arranged to meet a friend for a whole day of retail therapy. It made a real change from trying to get round the shops at super speed in order to avoid irritating my bored bloke. Instead of enduring a running commentary of: 'This is hell on earth', 'Do you really want it that badly?', 'Look at that queue!' – I actually had a nice time. My friend and I perused the shops at leisure, broke off for a boozy lunch and then continued drooling over dresses, shoes, make-up and soft furnishings without one single sarcastic comment. Bliss! We also made a point of hiring a beauty therapist to come to one of our homes once a month to give us massages and facials.

'But these things cost money,' I hear you say. Well, it doesn't need to cost the earth and there are plenty of worthwhile things you can do to fill your time that cost very little or nothing at all. You could volunteer to help a charity, bake cakes, make your own greeting cards or join a dance class. It's all too easy to see little parts of yourself fade away in a relationship. Nights out and spa days with the girls are swapped for takeaways and TV. Or your love for far-flung holidays exploring the jungle is replaced by yearly trips to the beach in Spain because he just doesn't 'do' adventure.

Whatever it was, becoming single again is the chance for you to remember who *you* are, to remind yourself what you loved about your life before him. You were happy before, and you will be again, so take time to think about what you really enjoyed doing, and then force yourself to go and do it, no matter how scary it seems.

You may even find that being single inspires you to go off and have adventures on your own. One friend, Sunny, often plans solo trips abroad and always comes back with amazing stories of the people she's met and the things she's seen.

While Sunny uses her holidays to take time out, reflect on life and celebrate her independence, another friend,

Jasmine, went travelling to get over her heartache and found the experience very cathartic. She now cites jetting off to new and exciting climes as the best thing she ever did after her boyfriend Lee went for the jugular in breaking her heart.

'His pièce de résistance was telling me I wasn't "the marrying type",' she says. 'It was probably the most hurtful thing you could say to a girl who has always dreamt about getting married and having children. But there was no way I was going to sit around and wallow, so I decided to go travelling instead. Over the next three weeks, I secretly planned my future – I gave notice on my house and job, and applied for a visa.'

When a few weeks later Lee invited her out to dinner, Jasmine decided to tell him her plans.

'He actually cried,' she recalls. 'He said he couldn't believe I was leaving London but then announced he'd started seeing a girl from work. Cue tears from me too.'

So when she left London, Jasmine vowed to leave thoughts of Lee behind too. Now six months on and living the high life on the Australian Gold Coast, Jasmine says she is one hundred per cent over Lee.

'I have no pictures of him, no reminders or keepsakes, so it's like starting a new life as if he was never part of it. No one here knows anything about him and none of my friends has met him. Coming to Australia was definitely the best cure for a broken heart. There is no chance of bumping into him when I haven't done my make-up, no chance of seeing him look into the eyes of his new woman, and no chance of seeing his friends and pretending that I'm fine.

'Being abroad makes that relationship seem so trivial in

comparison to what I now have: new friends, a new dream job, sunshine everyday and lots of hunky surfers to look at! Not to mention the fact that I'm now dating my gorgeous personal trainer.'

Obviously, there are some occasions when you just can't get away from the undesirable who broke your heart. While having him out of sight does help to push him out of your mind, it is still completely possible to get over him while you continue to see him.

The simple fact is you have to get over him. What else can you do? Sit and bawl from the sidelines as he gets on with his life, gets a new girlfriend, gets married, has kids and your life passes you by? I think not! It's time to embrace your exciting single status.

What I love about single life

'You don't have to feel bad if you want to spend an entire weekend sitting on the couch, eating chocolate and ice cream and watching chick-flicks. That's what you're supposed to do when you're single. Live the cliché and enjoy it!'

'When I found a new job that meant moving a hundred miles away I didn't have to take anyone else's opinion into consideration in deciding if I should take it.'

'Never having to ask permission to do something, not having to tell anyone where you are or when you're coming home. You can flirt and be cheeky. The world is your oyster.'

'I like never having to feel jealous if he chats to a girl for more than five minutes. No matter how self-confident you are, there's always that little seed of doubt. Does he fancy her more than me? Why doesn't he pay me that much attention? Of course, most of the time it's nothing, but being single again means you don't even have to think about it. That does wonders for your self-esteem.'

'If you've been left wounded by your ex, there's nothing better than getting a bit of attention from a male admirer, whether it's five seconds of flirting in the supermarket or just an appreciative glance as a stranger walks past.'

'The best thing about being single can be summed up in one word – freedom. Suddenly, people start telling you how lucky you are to be able to go anywhere and do anything you like at any time. And when you stop feeling sorry for yourself and realise they're right, it's a great feeling.'

'It's great to know that you're going to fall in love

again. You're going to experience that knee-wobbling, heart-pounding butterflies feeling that comes with meeting a new man that could, just maybe, be Mr Right.'

'You're allowed to kiss as many frogs as you like until you find the right one.'

'As you get older, you find the number of single women among your friends dwindling to almost nothing, so I was terrified when I suddenly found myself on my own and in my mid-thirties. I thought that was it, I'd be forgotten and left on the shelf for good, but I wasn't. In fact, I found myself feeling like the most desirable woman in every room. Often, as the only single woman, I was surrounded by similarly available men. Perfect!'

'Getting to snog guys who you were dying to kiss when you were attached, but couldn't. Oh, and actually taking some pride in your appearance again. Whilst you can convince yourself that your boyfriend will/should love you regardless of how gross you look, new potentials may not have the same attitude!'

'You can be selfish without feeling guilty and do whatever you want without having to put someone else first.'

6.
How to ditch a no-hoper

Sitting in my car with a sulky look on my face, I listened to the words that I didn't want to hear. 'You can't have me,' Ciaran, the elusive charmer, told me with a smirk. 'I'm not on the market.'

I'd already wasted a good two months of my life seeing Ciaran and the prognosis hadn't been good from the start. First, he'd failed to mention he had a girlfriend. Then, when I did find out, he had the audacity to kick me out of his house at 7.30 a.m. because she was on her way round. Add to this the fact that he'd wolf-whistled at my flatmate as she crossed the road and then laughed unashamedly when I told him I knew about it, and you're beginning to get the picture.

'Very attractive girl, that Naomi,' he'd said by way of explanation. Riiiiiight.

So, any sensible girl would be running, screaming for the hills at full-pelt, desperate to put as much distance as possible between this man and herself, yes? Yet for some reason I was still pathetically continuing to crave his attention as he spelt it out that while our 'arrangement' could continue, there was no way I had girlfriend credentials.

I know what you're thinking: bummer, huh? He sounds like such a catch. And don't even get me started on the guilt. By this point I knew he had a girlfriend, but there simply wasn't any room in my head to think of her feelings, I was just too caught up in him.

Whenever the thought of her did cross my mind, I tried to shove it into a corner, desperate to pretend – though I knew I was fooling myself – that we belonged together and he'd soon realise it. What I should have realised was that he wasn't worth another second of my precious time, or his poor girlfriend's.

But, no matter how many times I found myself being treated as a second-class citizen, I just let him get away with it, crying myself to sleep and thinking something about me was wrong. So why was I allowing myself to be treated in this despicable way?

It wasn't doing my street cred any favours – my house-mates made no attempt to hide the fact they loathed him, all my friends said he sounded like an arse, and he himself as good as admitted that he was using me – yet I continued to chase him around like a lap dog.

I'd weep at night because he had no respect for me, but I had no respect for myself. You see, as much as I'd unwittingly stumbled into a no-hoper situation, I should have ended it the moment I discovered about the girlfriend or the wolf-whistle or the fact that he was 'off the market'. The way the situation had panned out meant that he held all the cards, and didn't he just know it. He could treat me any way he wanted and I would just take it. And, in a slightly warped way, this amused him.

I've found that some guys can be like this. If they even get a sniff that you're really keen (or know you're interested, when they're not), it's almost as if they become small boys again. The sort of schoolboys who probably enjoyed sprinkling salt on slugs or using magnifying glasses to fry ants in the sunshine. The sort of vile little toerags who used to stalk around the playground cornering sensitive souls like me and tearing them to shreds with their incessant teasing.

A friend, Eddie, has sheepishly admitted that, rather than break up with girls who fail to impress him, he'll often deliberately antagonise them to see what he can get away with. He realises his behaviour is abhorrent, but it's as if he has a sadistic urge to challenge the unfortunate lady in question to step up and put him in his place.

In Eddie's most recent instance of torment, he very maturely got drunk on a pub crawl and decided it was time for the girl he'd been dating to know just how annoying he found her.

'She was just a bit wet,' he says. 'When I'm drunk I can be an ass, so because she was irritating me, I started asking all these inappropriate questions to wind her up, including if she'd ever wondered what human flesh tasted like. Unsurprisingly, she was really hurt and kept asking me over and over again why I was doing it.'

Thankfully, Eddie's now not-so-smitten squeeze was not about to let such pathetic behaviour go unpunished and she soon put him in his place very publicly.

'She told me it was over,' he reveals. 'Then she told all her friends in the pub how I'd behaved. By the time we'd clambered on to the bus to head for the next drinking hole, all her friends were chanting, "Eddie is a wanker! Eddie is a wanker!" In the end I couldn't take any more so I got off to escape them. At that point I decided it was best for me to cut my losses and walk home. A richly deserved come-uppance, I think – full power to her.'

So, the twisted thing is that after deliberately sabotaging the romance, Eddie actually respected his long-suffering ex for standing up to him – but by then she was long gone. Nice guy, Eddie.

But at least his girlfriend had the good sense to tell him to take a hike when his behaviour got too bad – far too many of us get trapped in relationships in which we make excuses for the other person. Often, he'll start taking advantage or treating you badly in just a minor way, making you think it's just a one-off and he won't do it again. But then, of course, he does something a little bit worse and you make an excuse for him once more.

You might even convince yourself that he loves you, really, and will soon realise this isn't the way to treat you. But the longer you let him get away with it, the more miserable you'll be and the more often he'll keep doing it. Why would he bother to change if you let him treat you just the way he wants to, regardless of your feelings?

If a man likes you, then he should treat you nicely – not actively belittle you with shoddy excuses or callous behaviour. While there is no doubt that girls like to be kept on their toes, there is a big difference between the guy who reels you in with an air of mystery and the man who takes you for a complete mug. If he is conducting himself like the Ciarans and Eddies of this world, there's no point hanging on in there and hoping for the best. Ditch the no-hoper and move on.

In a nice conclusion, when I finally cut my losses with Ciaran (after the slow realisation that he was never going to leave his girlfriend for me) and wisely ceased all contact in order to get over him, I did get my opportunity to put him in his place.

It was six months later, by which time he had split up with his girlfriend (oh, the irony), when I spied him drunkenly snogging the face off an equally paralytic girl in a pub. With his usual charm, the minute he clocked me, he dropped her like a hot potato and sidled over. After acting sleazy and telling me how 'well' I looked, he gave me his business card and told me to call him later so we could 'have a party back at his'.

Seizing my moment, I smiled sweetly then ripped the card up and dropped the pieces on the floor. It felt good. It was as if I was seeing him for the first time now that I was out of my 'but I love him' stupor. At last, instead of making excuses for him, I could see he was not even close to being good enough for me.

Of course, sometimes, a total lack of respect radiates off a new suitor within the first few dates, as Mary discovered with our next flaky fella, Nigel.

'He was a bit of an oddity,' explains Mary. 'We'd been on a couple of dates when I spotted him in my local pub. Rather than rush over, I wanted to play it cool so I sent my friend to the bar. It was nearing 11 p.m. so everyone was quite plastered, but I really was shocked to see Nigel homing in on my friend at the bar. She was very drunk and he wouldn't let her escape. Then the next thing I knew they were kissing!

'Furious with both of them, I stormed out of the bar – apparently just before she threw up all over him and he took her home.' Nice.

Next on our no-hoper hit list is bachelor boy Bryan whose constant mixed messages drove Alicia up the wall.

'We first met at a party where we were introduced by a friend of a friend,' Alicia reveals. 'We hit it off, swapped numbers and met up. It was then he told me that he wanted to be single. "OK," I agreed. It was only our first date, after all.'

But Bryan kept texting and calling Alicia, so eventually she agreed to have dinner with him. 'It was all very pleasant,' she adds. 'But, true to form, over our mains he told me that he wanted to be single. I actually said, "OK, fine, be single!"

'A few nights later, he turned up in my local bar, flirted with me and walked me home. I bid him farewell and headed upstairs to my flat, but just as I walked in, my phone started to ring. It was Bryan saying that he was still outside and could I come back down.'

Dutifully Alicia trotted back downstairs to find Bryan with a masterful look on his face. 'I knew I'd regret it if I didn't come back and do this,' he announced. Then, like a brooding hero from a Jane Austen novel, he swept her up for a passionate embrace.

When Bryan had finished kissing a swoony Alicia, he had something else to say. Yes, you've guessed it – that he wanted to be single.

'By this point I just wanted to scream,' rants Alicia. 'It was worse than a scene from a bad rom-com movie. A few days later, he texted me about going for a drink – the same day that I spotted he'd changed his Facebook status to "in a relationship". Sick to the back teeth of his mind games, I deleted the text and decided to move on.'

While Alicia had the right idea, so often we can't (or don't want to) see the wood for the trees and find ourselves believing what we want to believe.

The ridiculous excuses we give to justify why he hasn't called

'He hasn't called me in three weeks because he doesn't want to seem too eager. Yeah. He's so into me, he's ignoring me.'

'Maybe he didn't pack his charger. That must be why he hasn't been in touch since he went on his lads' holiday in Tenerife.'

'He must be running scared because he thinks I'm so special and he doesn't want to mess things up by being too keen.'

'Maybe something terrible has happened to him? Perhaps he has been mugged and had his phone stolen.'

'My phone can't be working — I'd better check it every thirty seconds. This means he'll be getting an engaged tone every time he tries, which clearly explains the non-call. I bet he's actually been trying to call the whole time!'

'He's in a ditch after crashing his car (whilst trying to text me). I then imagine a policeman answering the phone as it rings beside his lifeless body. Overactive imagination, moi?'

I'm sad to report that after all this wonderful creative thinking, the prognosis just isn't very good. When I asked a bunch of guys why men don't call when they say they will, the results were damning.

'We're just too cowardly to say we don't fancy the girl,' one admitted. 'We lie in order to finish a date or sexual encounter without you making a scene,' another justified. In a crushing crescendo, a third added, 'We're just not callous enough to say, "No, I will not be calling you because you're not good-looking enough and I don't find your conversation stimulating." You wouldn't kick a puppy, would you?' Charming!

And, just in case you wondered, the general consensus appeared to be that if he really, really likes you, he'll be in touch within two days. But if it hasn't happened in a week, you should make alternative dinner plans. One guy adds, 'After two weeks, be assured that if a guy calls or texts at this late stage, it's because he's having a confidence crisis and is looking to reassure himself.' Ouch.

So, if he's not calling or not making an effort to meet up, then ignoring the obvious just prolongs the inevitable, as Caroline discovered . . .

'When I first went on a couple of dates with Myles, a guy I'd met through mutual friends, it looked promising,' she recalls. 'He seemed keen and asked for a third date – something we arranged for the following Saturday night.'

On the morning of their date day, full of high hopes for the evening ahead, an excited Caroline went out and bought a gorgeous new frock. Then she headed home to get ready.

'At 4 p.m., I called him, as we'd arranged, to see what time he wanted to meet,' she explains. 'But when Myles answered the phone, he didn't sound at all enthusiastic. He told me that he was still at his friend's place, having been wasted the night before. He promised he would go home, have a sleep and call me when I woke up.'

But by 9 p.m. there was still no word and a furious fuchsia-frocked Caroline was at home necking wine with angry abandon. 'After polishing off half a bottle of wine, I finally called him,' she says. 'It only rang three times before he clearly cancelled my call. How rude!'

You'd think that after such ungentlemanly behaviour Caroline might find a sorry suitor on her doorstep the next day pleading forgiveness. But, alas, the following twenty-four hours brought nothing of the sort. There was no begging phone call, no regretful text, not a sausage. Desperately, she racked her brain for some sort of plausible explanation and thus created the following:

A. 'He fell asleep and was too embarrassed to call me.'

B. 'He is waiting for my birthday on Saturday and will send me a huge bunch of flowers.'

C. 'He is a cheeky bugger who doesn't give a shit about standing me up.'

To an outsider, it was all too clear which of her explanations was most likely to be correct. Surely, if Myles really liked her, he'd be prepared to put in a reasonable amount of effort to treat her right at the beginning of their courtship? But the problem was that previously he had been nice to Caroline, so naturally his overnight change of behaviour dumbfounded her.

Like so many of us do, she felt she clearly needed to investigate further to discover his true inner fuckwit. And that is what came to pass. Bemused by Myles' silence, Caroline included him on the round robin email for her birthday party the following Friday. She justified her actions as being an opportunity for Myles to redeem himself. And to her credit, her email bait worked.

'On the day of the party, he called to apologise and said he'd avoided ringing as he felt so bad,' she says sheepishly. 'I wanted to give him what for, but immediately felt my resolve waning. Of course, when he turned up at the party I ended up kissing him.'

It was clear that Caroline needed some kind of short, sharp shock to highlight why Myles was not worth her time or effort. This came when he invited her to his house party the following night, on her actual birthday.

'At first, he was all over me,' reveals Caroline. 'But then a very attractive South African girl turned up. Suddenly, he was off showing her round his place and, as they started to make eyes at each other, it was very predictable what was going to happen next. Lo and behold, while a few of us were in his bedroom, he sneaked her into his housemate's room.'

Indeed, dear Myles was such a class act that he conducted his brief encounter with the door half-open, then headed back to the party, leaving his bewildered conquest to get dressed.

At which point, thankfully, Caroline had realised just how great an escape she'd had. 'I spent the rest of the evening ignoring him and getting drunk with his mates,' she says. 'Then later, I heard the South African girl complaining that he was now ignoring her. I actually had a great night in the end and was thoroughly relieved that I'd finally seen him in his true colours.'

We don't like to say it, but we told you so!

While Myles' cad credentials appear clear-cut, most of us can sympathise with being in a situation similar 'But he's nice some of the time', I hear you justify. 'Maybe I just need to give him a chance.'

But this is where it all gets a bit tricky.

As one man explains, 'The rule of blossoming relationships is that men show they are keen by pretending they're not. We know only too well that if we act too enthusiastically women feel suffocated.'

But, and this is a big but, he agrees that playing it cool is very different from playing it downright mean. 'While the bloke that plays it cool probably has his eye on the end game, there's a big difference between that and treating you like shit,' he adds. 'So while a guy might forget to call accidentally-on-purpose a couple of times to keep you on your toes, he would never stand you up if he liked you – that's just rude!'

So, yes, it's tempting to ride the storm for a while – to stay with the run-around rogue and see if he comes good. But it's all about boundaries – if you express that you are unhappy with his unpredictable behaviour and he then makes an effort to redeem himself, then fair enough.

So next time you find yourself being led down the garden path by a man who promised to call but didn't, then asked you out but was a no-show, then, finally, when he took you out, lavished you with attention and is now back at yours wrestling with your top and trying to get his leg over, just be on your guard.

In fact why not ditch the eejit and I'll introduce you to this nice chap instead.

'When I'm utterly committed to a relationship I don't cancel plans 'cause I'm a bit wrecked,' Justin says. 'I will meet up even if I am bleeding from the eyes. Two years ago, I had a septic foot and was in hospital with serious blood poisoning, yet I discharged myself to see my then girlfriend's opening night of her new play.

'When I'm utterly committed, I tell the girl I love her every day, and if I don't see her, I text her. So easy to do, and pays MASSIVE dividends.'

Ahhh.

* * *

Of course, girls often put up with bad behaviour at the beginning of a romance merely because we don't want to be labelled 'psychos' or 'bunny boilers' (damn Glenn Close for cursing us all). We are scared to raise grievances for fear of the relationship failing, and carry on miserably in the hope that one day he'll realise what a good thing he's got. But after years of being a sap and allowing myself to put up with disrespectful behaviour, I now have to disagree with this method of conducting a courtship.

I've learnt the hard way that if you give him an inch, he'll probably take a mile. Did any of the men who treated me horrendously come good in the end? Nope. They either dumped me or I walked away long after I should have, feeling like the world's biggest pushover.

By continuing to allow mistreatment, you are doing yourself a disservice – when all the while you could be out there meeting nice, respectful fellows.

But just how do you separate the wheat from the chaff? Which suitors will reap rich rewards and which bad seeds are dead in the ground? If you can dissect the signs, then you've got a head start on all of us.

He's a lost cause: the signs (as dictated by men)

'When we're attempting to shake you off, we never finish a text or email with a question as that would be inviting a response – which we don't want.'

'It depends on the situation, but if we look away when you smile at us, or talk about somebody else when you come on to us, they are both big clues that you're wasting your time.'

'Unfortunately, the signs that I'm not interested are the same as the ones when I get shy and am really interested in you. Odd that.'

'If there's no eye contact and he's not laughing at your jokes, then it ain't happening.'

'If he's not calling as often to ask you out, or there's less contact or general avoidance, then you've had it.'

'Guys are not particularly subtle creatures. You know we are not interested because we do things that uninterested people do.'

'Most men will never slam a door, they'll always leave it slightly ajar. You never know when you're going to find yourself a little drunk, bored, lonely and in that girl's neck of the woods.'

'If we never return a call, cancel on you or are slow to respond, then we're just not that bothered.'

'Before the first date, not texting and calling can be

> put down to the man playing it cool and observing
> dating rules of not looking too keen. However, after
> having been out together, if he is then not texting or
> calling, you can safely assume he wasn't blown away
> by the date.'
>
> 'Just remember, the men of today are not far removed
> from their caveman ancestors. We go in for the chase,
> get our wicked way, and then if you have no person-
> ality, you're history, and it's on to the next one.'

And with that little insight into the great male mind, I can now see half my adult lifetime trickling into a dustbin labelled 'wasted hours obsessing over flaky boys'. Ho hum.

Of course, he might not be uninterested or flaky or manipulating your mind with mixed messages – he could just be completely unavailable.

A good few years ago I was asked out by a handsome man who was about ten years older than me. He took me on a couple of really nice dates and on the second, after kissing him for what seemed like an age, I suddenly had an overwhelming urge to ask him if he'd ever been married. Perhaps it was a sixth sense because suddenly he looked shamefaced.

'Are you married right now?' I gasped.

'Er . . .,' he replied.

It was then that he revealed that not only was he married and in the 'middle' of breaking up with his wife, but he also had an eight-month-old daughter. Of course, he was adamant that the marriage was dead and buried and he wanted a whole new life. It was obvious that he viewed me as his escape route. If he launched into a full-on affair, it would give him a purpose and there would be no going back.

But I didn't want to be responsible for breaking up a marriage or stealing a father away from an eight-month-old baby, so I told him we wouldn't be seeing each other again. Yes, it was tempting to believe that his marriage was over, but it also seemed sad that he'd give up on everything he had so easily. Then, about a year later, I got an email from him out of the blue. 'I'm back with my wife,' he admitted. 'We're much happier now and I'm glad you told me to give it another chance.'

I was glad too.

If I hadn't been so sensible things could have become very messy, and likely as not, we'd all have ended up with broken hearts. Being someone's way out of a relationship is only going to end badly.

They'll stick with you until they're free of the other person, but what happens then? More often than not, you'll be dropped like a hot potato and you'll realise you were just the in-between girl – not something anyone ever wants to be. So save yourself the heartbreak and drama. As a rule, if the man who is pursuing you is married or in a relationship, then he should be viewed automatically as a no-hoper.

While there are exceptions to the rule (one of my good friends found her perfect match in the work colleague who left his wife for her), generally it's best to steer clear. After all, conducting courtships is difficult enough without all that extra baggage involved. Why make life any harder for yourself?

Sometimes, the realisation it's all over strikes you like a thunderbolt. There's an instant of stark clarity where his no-hoper credentials hit you like a blast from a Taser gun. After playing with the idea of finishing with him in your head, suddenly one defining moment, no matter how big or small, spurs you into action, as Dinah found.

'The day after the September 11 terrorist attack was Greg's birthday,' she reveals. 'As a treat, I was supposed to be turning up with an Indian takeaway, but I discovered on going round to our usual restaurant that it had unexpectedly closed down.

'Consequently, I was late, he was starving and he gave me the full-on strop treatment when I finally got there with an alternative Indian meal. You can imagine my rant: "Thousands of people have died, jumped out of office blocks and their families' lives are ruined, and all you can think about is your sodding stomach!" It really was the straw that broke the camel's back and we broke up the following day.'

The moment the death knell sounded

'I decided I'd had enough when he erupted because I left the tap on while I brushed my teeth. The same guy wouldn't even let me borrow a vase at his house for flowers a friend had bought for me, so they sat for a week in his sink. I could go on.'

'One boyfriend had a billionaire dad and we were due to go and stay in his parents' Cape Town beach house. But the thought of two weeks solid in his company was just too much – so I dumped him. Giving up a holiday in South Africa – that's how irritating he was.'

'One ex told me that I thought I was Paris Hilton, which makes me laugh to this day. That definitely was the nail in the coffin for me!'

'I once dumped a guy because one of his front teeth got knocked out, and then I saw him wearing some really awful sandals.'

'I had an argument with my ex about how one should go about blending a Cadbury's Cream Egg. That was kind of it for us.'

'My ex's birthday was on a cold December morning and he threw a massive wobbly because I dressed to go to work in trousers and not a tight skirt. He asked me to change, I said no, and there began the argument to end all arguments – we had a physical fight and he went off and spent his birthday in a pub getting hammered. Finito.'

'One boyfriend told me, "You love your monkey more than me." Although he's very cute, there was really no need to be jealous of a stuffed toy.'

'On our first date, he offered to cook. When I got there I saw he'd bought out the entire discount section from the supermarket and was now creating a meal around it. I decided then and there he was just too tight.'

So there you go – despaired at, dispatched and discarded.

Over the course of this book we've heard numerous accounts about contemptible conduct from caddish creatures, but let's not be hypocritical. At this very point in time men everywhere are licking their sore wounds after a beastly encounter with a femme fatale. They might not shout about it or attempt to extract revenge in the way we often do, but they are certainly feeling it, downing pints with disgust, and secretly listening to ELO's 'Evil Woman' on their iPods.

There's just no escaping that girls can be pretty abominable too, as Louise, one such offender, concedes: 'I'm so bad at breaking up,' she says. 'So after a two-year on-off long-distance relationship, I moved flat and changed my phone number without telling him.'

While Louise viewed this as a 'no messing' termination of their relationship, you can only imagine the pain this caused the young man in question. Was there really any need to make it quite that brutal? But that's the thing about instigating a break-up – you can dress it up any way you like, but it's all about being selfish.

When good girls go bad

'I broke up with my boyfriend five days after we returned from our summer holiday. I knew before we went that it was over, but I kept telling people that it was a "make or break" trip. For most of the holiday, I kept my head in a book on the beach. When we got back, I finished it and the book.'

'I'd been going out with Carl for eighteen months when I decided to end it with him over the phone. He cried and I felt bad because I wasn't upset. Then my sister came into the room to tell me to hurry up because we were going out. When she heard me say, "I'll miss you too", she started laughing and mouthing "no you won't!" which made me want to laugh. Then she turned around, pulled down her trousers and started mooning me while I was trying to console a crying Carl. I was trying to be sincere and not laugh while I had an arse in my face, but instead I started sniggering. I've always felt bad about that.'

'I'd just moved into a new house with my boyfriend

Tut-tut girls.

But just like the men we've lambasted, such cowardly behaviour often results in lily-livered ladies getting their just desserts – which is something Amelia discovered in a perfect tale of poetic justice.

'I was working as a waitress in Southampton when I began a romance with a barman who worked in a nearby pub,' she says. 'Craig and I were seeing each other on and off for a couple of months, but then I went to France to do a ski season. He expressed an interest in visiting me and, not really thinking it would happen, I told him he was welcome at any time.'

Fast-forward a couple of months and Amelia was on a roll, having managed to pull most of the blokes at her ski resort. It was at this point that Craig got in touch to say he was coming to visit.

'It was the last thing I wanted,' admits Amelia. 'So when he kept ringing and ringing, I didn't take his phone calls. Then he emailed and said he'd booked a flight leaving in two weeks' time. Panic-stricken, I immediately called him and told him he couldn't come as I'd broken my arm and might have to head home. Despite his insistence that he'd still fly over to look after me, I snapped that he just couldn't. I think in the end he knew what was really going on, and I never heard from him again.'

With her problem solved, a smug Amelia put on her finest salopettes, grabbed her snowboard and sauntered off to the slopes, wiggling her pert behind at any handsome man she spotted en route. Then, as she glided effortlessly down a black run, she took a tumble and broke her wrist. As she herself admits, 'If that's not come-uppance, I don't know what is!'

And so to our last tale of crime and retribution . . .

When Vivian decided to dump her boyfriend, she wasn't really that concerned about how he'd feel. 'It wasn't really working with Gabriel and, to be honest, I just wanted to cut my losses and get out of there,' she says. 'So, knowing that I was going to break up with him, I craftily waited until he'd given me a ride home from a party on his motorcycle before I did the deed.

'When we arrived, I jumped off and really couldn't be bothered to dress it up, so told him very bluntly it was over. I then stormed up the steps to my apartment building. Job done.

'It was only when I got inside that I realised I was still wearing his motorbike helmet. So, shamefully, I then had to slope back downstairs and hand it to him. He was there waiting patiently, with a smirk on his face. I guess he got the last laugh.'

The problem with break-ups is that when one person wants out, it is rarely pain free. If you have been with someone for a long time and were seemingly in love, you can't avoid hurting them when you end it. In your mind, you have slowly been processing thoughts about leaving them and starting a new life, but they haven't – they are being hit with the news you no longer want them, often with absolutely no warning.

As one man revealed, 'The very worst thing is being blindsided and broken up with out of the blue. It leads to paranoia in every subsequent relationship.'

Which is something to consider when you are planning a moonlit flit. Unfortunately, Denise was already engaged to be married when she decided she wanted a fresh start.

'I just couldn't envisage marrying my fiancé Michael,' she reveals. 'Or telling him I felt that way. So I began to hatch a plan. I would leave our flat in Aldershot and move back to my home town of Leicester. I told myself that by getting everything in place and then walking out as soon as I'd told him it was over, I would cause him the minimal amount of heartache.

'So I carefully timed the break-up for when the lease on our flat would be up and secretly handed in my notice at work. I then conspired with my mum over email to find a flat back in Leicester. I also circulated my CV to various recruitment firms to line up a new job.'

As D-Day approached, Denise carried on as normal. But it was one Saturday night, as she hit the town with girlfriends, that she came unstuck. As she was giggling with her pals in her favourite wine bar, she suddenly saw a sombre figure approaching. It was Michael.

'He looked terrible,' she adds. 'He was crying and shaking, and I knew I'd been rumbled. It turned out he'd hacked into my Hotmail account and had read every single email plotting my escape.'

As they left the bar and headed towards the taxi rank, Michael announced he wanted to walk. Unfortunately, this was the night Denise had chosen to christen a brand new pair of four-inch stilettos.

'My feet were killing me, but I knew I wasn't in a position to argue,' she adds. So, reluctantly, I shuffled and winced down the main road towards our home. Meanwhile, Michael cried and shouted at me for the entire forty-minute journey. By the time we got home, both my feet were bleeding, but I didn't dare complain. With my big plan foiled, I packed my stuff and left the next day.'

How to finish it with dignity

While Denise didn't mean to hurt Michael (and he shouldn't have hacked into her emails), perhaps it would have been best if she'd simply broken up with him and moved in with a friend until all the other arrangements were in place.

In her eyes, the plan backfired because Michael read her emails – but even if she'd had the chance to feed him a nice watered-down version, it probably would have seemed cold and calculating anyway. He'd still have faced the reality that she'd planned a whole new life without him, all the while pretending that everything was fine and dandy.

The difficulty is that breaking up *is* a sticky business and there will inevitably be casualties along the way, but you need to be brave and take responsibility for what you're doing. If you're breaking up with your boyfriend, you need to give him the opportunity to ask questions and hear your explanations. And with this comes a massive responsibility – the speed at which he bounces back and his future happiness will be influenced by what you hit him with right now.

Don't tell him the truth to make yourself feel less guilty if it'll hurt him more. Do you really need to proportion blame or admit you've already got your eye on someone else? Sometimes a lie can be kinder. But don't draw it out either. It may seem a nicer option to let someone down gradually. But false hope is not going to help him get to grips with the fact that the relationship has come to an end; it just makes the pain and uncertainty last longer.

Indeed, it can prove very dicey indeed, as Gail discovered.

'I'd been dating Terry, a rather fiery and possessive lawyer, for three months and knew he wasn't The One,' she says. 'So I hatched a plan to move to Dubai after being offered an exciting new job on a magazine. But when he announced, "I'd better pack my shorts", I realised he thought he was coming too.

'I wanted to break up with him, but with all the upheaval of moving countries, I just wasn't brave enough to tell him. It all seemed like too much to cope with.'

But, predictably, the situation snowballed. Terry kept telling all his friends and family that they were moving to Dubai and things were getting increasingly awkward. So Gail bit the bullet and told him.

'I sat him down and explained that I would be moving to Dubai by myself,' she says. 'He was beside himself and stormed out. I carried on packing, relieved that it was finally over.'

On the day of the big move, Gail was loading the last of her belongings into a taxi to the airport, when Terry appeared from nowhere and jumped in next to her.

'He was begging me to give us another chance and to allow him to join me in Dubai,' she says. 'It was horrendous! In the end, I hugged him goodbye in Departures, and he stood there crying, as I went through the sliding doors to Customs, cutting off our relationship for good. I will never forget the poignant picture of six-foot-tall Terry, with tears streaming down his face, but it felt as though I was walking through a Narnia-style wardrobe to a new and exciting life.'

Poor Terry, but at least he heard it face to face.

I think we all know that ending it with someone by email or phone or in a text is simply not befitting a lady. The location and point at which you tell him has got to be right too.

'For some inexplicable reason I chose to break up with my boyfriend Lewis at my place and last thing at night,' reveals Tabitha. 'Unfortunately, he had no friends nearby so we had no choice but to share the same single bed.' So, with a blotchy-eyed truce and weary with emotional exhaustion, they wedged themselves into Tabitha's tiny bed for the night.

The following morning, after more tears, a heartbroken Lewis walked out and a wretched Tabitha fled to weep on her friend's shoulder. It was at that point she realised with panic that Lewis had the only keys to her flat.

'Unfortunately he didn't have a mobile and I didn't know where he'd gone,' she reveals. 'I had no idea if he was grabbing a bus or train or just wandering around weeping. So I had to chase around trying to find him.

'When I did finally spot him at the train station, I ran up to him in a complete panic. After all the emotion of the past few days, I think he thought I was going to tell him I'd made a huge mistake. Unfortunately, I then had to break his heart all over again by asking for my keys back. I'm surprised he didn't throw them at me!'

It's not nice hurting someone, but if it just can't be avoided, there are a couple of other ways you can do right by him. First, you could discreetly tell a friend of his that they might need to be on hand, and secondly, you can leave him alone. If he does call begging you to take him back, be firm but not unkind. We all know what it's like to be in that sort of heartbroken hell, frantically clutching at straws.

There are times when niceties go out the window – but only in extreme circumstances.

Janey had a dilemma. She had been going out with a guy she'd met at college for several weeks. He was super keen and she wasn't. Even worse, he was the cousin of her sister's fiancé, so she was worried about how to end it without upsetting her sibling's intended. But at the same time, he was really beginning to irritate her.

Thankfully, the holidays arrived and she took a summer

job miles away, and she hoped he wouldn't bother to stay in touch. But he did, obviously envisaging a romantic reunion.

In an unexpected twist, a nasty case of glandular fever came to her aid (probably instigated by kissing a bronzed surfer). She was so ill she had to return early and couldn't bear the thought of her boyfriend's misplaced concern. Weak with illness, she scrawled a Dear John note in pencil on a tatty piece of paper and asked her mother to post it to him. It did the trick, as she didn't hear from him again.

While Janey's boyfriend accepted his fate, sometimes the message doesn't quite filter through. If he can't comprehend that it's over, then you could be in stalker territory. It's time to keep your curtains firmly closed and start screening your calls . . .

Stalk this way

'When I broke up with Andy, he seemed to take it all right, but the next day, as I was walking through town, I realised people were staring at me. When I turned around quickly, there he was – he'd been following me the whole time, flitting from lamp-post to telegraph pole. Then, the next day at work, I opened the blinds and saw him immediately, crouched on the footpath outside. He immediately ran away and, thankfully, I never saw him again!'

'When I told Jay that I'd prefer to be friends, he took it extremely badly. At first, I was bombarded by texts, phone calls and all the usual nonsense, but when he went quiet I thought he'd got over it. That is, until I ran into him in a bar a few weeks later and he unbuttoned his shirt. There across his heart was my name "Alice" – a permanent tattoo. I told him categorically that there was no future for us. I heard later that he'd managed to adapt it to "MAlice".'

'When I was sixteen, my very first boyfriend Ade wooed me with the opening gambit "I'd never believed in love at first sight until I met you." But when soon after he started saying that he wanted a baby (we'd never even had sex!), I found that very weird and dumped him. He lived forty miles away so I didn't expect to see him again.

'Five years later, after a stint away at university, I was in my local supermarket when a security guard came over. It was Ade. Surprised to see him, I asked why he was working so far from where he lived. He then explained, with no hint of embarrassment, that he had taken a job near where I lived in the hope that I would shop there, and that he drove past my mum's house every day.

'As I stood there, gobsmacked, he added that he had a pregnant girlfriend but I only had to "say the word" and he would ask his boss for a break, call her

It's never too late

What's this I spy? A huddle of procrastinators? A gaggle of no-hoper hanger-on-ers? Let me guess. You've travelled so far down the weary break-up road that you feel completely numb? You don't have the energy to pull the plug, you're letting the relationship linger and there's never a right time? As Christine knows only too well, there's always a million reasons for you to avoid going through with it . . .

'I dated a guy for about three years, even though after twelve months I should have dumped him,' she admits. 'But there was always an excuse as to why I couldn't. Christmas, Valentine's Day or his birthday would be coming up, so surely it would be cruel to break up then? And if I dumped him at the beginning of summer, who would I go on bike rides, picnics and holidays with?

'The fact that he was also part of my group of friends didn't really help either. If I broke up with him, surely it would break the whole group up and my friends would hate me for ever. But when I finally did it, I felt so good. It was just having the guts to take the plunge.'

In an even worse scenario, when Susie wanted out she was not only engaged to Mike, but they'd also set the date and she'd bought the dress! As doubt set in, she watched each day fizzle away like a lighted fuse in the countdown to her wedding day.

'We got engaged after just six months, after which Mike became increasingly jealous and possessive,' she explains. 'On one occasion we had friends round for the evening and he was really drunk. When he started getting antagonistic, I asked his friends to leave.

'A few weeks later we went for dinner with my dad and my brother and throughout the meal I felt as though Mike was vying for my attention. True to form, on the way home he started slagging off my dad. There were so many instances like that, so one day I plucked up courage and just told him the wedding was off.'

Bizarrely, after their nuptials were cancelled, Susie and Mike's relationship ended without any fireworks, humiliation or sorrow. Instead, they split on the most amicable of terms.

'Poignantly, we finally broke up on the day we were supposed to get married,' Susie reveals. 'We'd marked the day by going for a picnic in the park together, and as we were enjoying a nice relaxing time I think we both realised we were more like mates. Later, we drove past the chapel where we were supposed to be getting married. I just felt nothing. When I asked Mike if he thought we'd ever get married, he replied that he didn't.

'As we agreed to go our separate ways, I waited to feel something, but it just didn't come. It was the least explosive break-up ever.'

So now for one final thing – don't ever go back!

'I broke up with my boyfriend Philip after he cheated on

me,' Wanda reveals. 'But thanks to a combination of loneliness and booze, I stupidly spent the night with him a couple of weeks later. We got back together and I instantly regretted it. Then the day I planned to break up with him, he told me his gran was dying.'

Not having the heart to add to his misery, Wanda decided to bide her time until Philip's grandmother passed away. With a respectable couple of weeks following the funeral under her belt, Wanda geared herself up once more. But, alas, tragedy struck a second time.

'This time Philip called to say his house had burnt down,' she reveals. 'How could I dump him when he was bloody homeless! So, reluctantly, I let him move in with me for a month, while he was finding somewhere to live.' But Philip's ungrateful attitude just cemented the fact that Wanda wanted him gone.

'The final straw was when he bought me a salt and pepper shaker for my birthday. I kicked him out and haven't seen him since.'

So, without further ado, set to it. If he's good, be firm, but kind. If he's bad, be harsh, but fair. And if he's a stalker, er, be careful.

And now you've finally done the deed, things are looking up. You're a free agent and there's a very exciting world out there.

7.

A crash course in single life

So let's move on to the crucial stuff – taking those first few baby steps out into the big bad world of single life. There's no escaping it – it's a bit of a wilderness out there. When you've just spent years in a relationship, suddenly you find yourself embarking on a crash course in the laws of the dating jungle.

Confusingly, the rules and methods of courtship are changing all the time. When I lived with three single girls in the days before mobile phones, it was a whole different ball game. We'd hit the town on Friday and Saturday night and sometimes would meet nice chaps. There would be drunken flirting and kissing and our communal phone number would be handed out.

It's hard to believe that just nine years ago mobile phones and emails hardly played a part in the dating game. Instead, you dutifully scribbled down your home telephone number and hoped for the best. Sunday mornings would see us congregating in the front room to watch the *Hollyoaks* omnibus and repeats of *Sunset Beach*. As we feasted on stodgy snacks, we'd swap stories from the night before and enjoy the heady feeling of still being a little bit drunk.

But by Sunday evening it would be a whole different

story. As PSD (post-session depression) began to set in, we'd all begin to feel a bit paranoid. Had we made idiots of ourselves and would so-and-so call? As each day passed and you waited for The Call, the perils of living in a house with three other single girls and just one landline became all too apparent.

Every time the phone rang we'd all tense up, trying our hardest to look nonplussed, then one of us would suddenly make a mad dash to get it. While the call was answered, the rest of us would stare ahead at the telly, frozen to the spot, but our ears twitching, straining to hear who was on the line. Then, as the inevitable 'Jackie, it's your mum!' rang out, all hope would be lost once more. Or, even worse, one of the other girls would hit the jackpot with a call from the man she'd met, while the rest of us felt slightly green and hard-done-by.

It actually must have been mighty hard to call our house. Without fail, one of us always seemed to be on the phone giggling to friends and clogging up the line. And it did jeopardise our chances. When I met a guy at a party, he asked a mutual friend for my number, but the call never came. Instead, months later, the friend revealed that he'd tried to call me on several occasions. But because the phone was constantly engaged, he'd apparently taken it as an omen that things were just not meant to be. Oh well, if he got put off at the first hurdle, he can't have liked me that much!

While having one phone line caused problems back then, at least it was simple. With so many ways to get in touch, it's all so complicated now. Do you call, text, email or do you use Messenger, Facebook or Twitter? Then there are all the different dating methods – do you speed date, Internet date, blind date or use the good old-fashioned bumping into a fit man in a bar technique?

I guess finding out what suits you kind of makes it fun. But never mind poking people on Facebook, what about some good old-fashioned romance? Wouldn't it be nice if life could be like the film *Serendipity* where you meet the love of your life by pure chance. Ahhh.

While that film is a load of sentimental old gobbledy-gook, there's no need to be cynical. Sometimes that kind of thing *does* happen in real life. If you look in the news-papers, the stories are there every day – the couple who met after she drove into the back of his car, the two strangers who made eyes at each other on the morning train, or the jurors who fell in love as they debated their verdict during a court case.

Then there's the couple who met when she called his phone number by accident, the guy who married the attractive girl he had spied parking nearby and had then left a post-it note on her window, and the man who saved a diabetic stranger from a hypoglycaemia attack and later proposed. So no need to be pessimistic!

You might not necessarily meet the man you'll spend the rest of your life with, but random opportunities should never be sniffed at, as Isobel discovered.

'One night, I'd been out to dinner with my dad when I got talking to a guy on the tube,' she reveals. 'In just two stops from Green Park to Pimlico, he'd persuaded me to go for a drink with him. So we left the tube, found a bar, had a drink and a sneaky snog, and then caught the last tube home. We've been going out ever since!'

One of the best things about single life is that even if your dates don't work out, are horrendously funny or simply spine-chilling, they will always make great stories for you to recount to your friends. Indeed, some of the funniest tales I've heard have come from girls who have come unstuck in some shape or form during their calamitous search for Mr Right.

Take Tara, who was completely oblivious when she hooked up with a bona fide member of the English aristocracy.

'I met the very drunken Charlie, who was wearing a full morning suit, after he had been drinking all day in the Royal Enclosure at Ascot. I thought he was a bit of an adorable romantic, so agreed to go back to his.'

Back at Charlie's pad it all looked a bit posh, and as he fetched her drink, Tara marvelled at pictures of him on a massive country estate and on shoots with stag heads and the like. 'After he'd shown me round, he basically charmed me into bed,' admits Tara. 'But his bloody dog slept at the end of the bed all night. It was like something out of a Jilly Cooper novel.'

The next morning, after promising that she would spend the weekend with him, Charlie kissed Tara goodbye. 'As I left, I was gobsmacked to see a letter on the doormat which had his full title on it,' she says. 'He was obviously quite the aristocrat – although his behaviour turned out to be anything but lordlike.

'A week later we arranged to go out to dinner and he blew me out by text just five minutes before he was due to pick me up.' Charming!

But while dates may go wrong, you should never underestimate the attraction of a girl who can laugh at herself – no matter how embarrassing the situation, as Stacy discovered.

'I was in the pub for my friend's birthday when we found ourselves talking to a really attractive guy,' she explains. 'It was one of those parties where everyone just got steaming drunk. There were shots of sambuca and tequila being passed around, and soon everyone was very inebriated.'

After chatting to her suave swain for some time, Stacy decided to make her way to the bar to replenish their drinks – and that is where she came unstuck. 'The area of the pub we were in was packed out, so I had to squeeze past some tables and lots of people to get up to the bar. When I came back clutching our drinks, I was really confused to see he was holding up an item of material that looked very like the wraparound skirt I was wearing.

'I think this might be yours,' he said with a grin.

At that moment, the full horror of what was happening suddenly dawned on Stacy. 'I realised I was in the middle of a crowded pub, in front of a guy I fancied in just my top and tights! Red-faced, but laughing, I quickly retrieved my skirt and tied it in a double knot.'

But all hope was not lost – even the sight of Stacy standing in her baggy Nora Batty granny tights didn't discourage her future paramour. Indeed, she pulled him later that night and ended up marrying him! You see, if you can just view the process of dating for what it should be – the chance to have lots of fun, then you can't go wrong.

Whether the attraction turns out to be there or not, there's no reason to view it all so seriously. It was during a date with a charismatic actor that I learned not to be so uptight. He'd asked me out a good month previously and we arranged to go to the theatre. But in the weeks that passed between our meeting and our first date, I met another guy I liked and had already been out with him a couple of times.

When I arrived to meet Sebastian, the actor, I immediately felt like a fraud. I felt nervous and knew I was very quiet and subdued. My body language was awkward and Sebastian was forced to do all the talking. He seemed bemused that having previously chatted all night, I now appeared to be mute. I've always been compelled to tell the truth, and as I sat there, I felt like the deception was stifling me. So, in the end, I just blurted it out in a really clumsy fashion. 'I don't want to lead you on,' I gabbled. 'I met him after you, so it wasn't intentional. I don't want to waste your time.'

But Sebastian clearly wasn't offended and actually laughed good-naturedly. 'It's fine,' he insisted. 'You don't need to worry about it. I'm seeing other people, too. I really didn't expect you to put everything on hold the minute you met me.' I actually felt a bit silly. It suddenly occurred to me that I was reading far too much into the situation. Why did it have to be so black and white?

After that, I found myself relaxing and Sebastian and I ended up having a really fun evening, chatting and laughing. There was no kiss at the end of the night, and I said goodbye knowing that we could go out any time and have a fantastic evening without the pressure or expectation of anything more than that.

The point is, when you are single, you can date lots of men without having to pull them. It doesn't have to be set in stone that you should fancy them, or take it further. Meeting new people and making good friends along the way is part of the fun.

But what if you do like the guy you're on a date with? What's the secret? How can you reel him in and then leave him hooked? You'd be surprised to know that less is actually more.

When I conducted my highly scientific research (*ahem*), most of the chaps I spoke to said a nice girl, who is ready to make an effort, but is also laid back and up for a laugh, would make the most appealing date. They also revealed that they care for things like a nice smile, sincerity in her eyes, confidence without arrogance, and a sense of style . . .

The desirable date wish list, as told by men

'She should laugh at your jokes, not count calories and look like she desperately wants to shag you at the end of the night.'

'If she's fun, funny and sexy, then she won't go wrong.'

'There should be no awkward silences, good chemistry and if she lets me eat some of her chips, then I'm sold.'

'She should be interesting and not stuck for things to say. She shouldn't be embarrassed about the situation either. You're both there for the same reason – to get to know one another.'

'I like a girl who will flirt, laugh and let you know that she likes you.'

'My ideal date is fun, interesting and smart. It's not rocket science, you just need to be interested in things.'

Now, without doubt, you have many of these lovely qualities – but what happens if you're cripplingly shy?

It's a ridiculous scenario: the first time you met him, he was simply introduced as a friend-of-a-friend, and you were your normal, animated self. You told him how you love dogs but are suspicious of cats, you waxed lyrical about *The Apprentice*, and even confessed that you secretly find Simon Cowell attractive. You know you had him captivated all night, but now you are meeting him on a date, you feel like you've lost your mojo. Suddenly, you know you will worry about everything that comes out your mouth; you will become obsessed with the fact that you might have something in your teeth, or that he'll spot that teeny-weeny pimple on your forehead.

My own dating demons appear when there's food involved. If there is ever a time when my clumsiness comes into full effect, it's when I am on a date. I'm lucky if I get through an evening without knocking my drink flying, dropping my knife on the floor or dripping sauce down my top. On a date, my food choices hinge entirely on how easy they are to manoeuvre from plate to mouth. I avoid high-risk fodder like spaghetti – there's just too much risk of it splashing or getting stuck to my chin.

I once went on a date with a rather rich and worldly man to a posh London eaterie, Nobu. It was all very nice, except that the food was Japanese and therefore eaten with chopsticks. Try as I might, I've never been able to master them. It's like giving a monkey a gun.

It was a terrible scenario for a first date. Haplessly, I attempted to shovel the morsels into my mouth, missing every time. To my utter mortification, a waitress took pity on me and offered me some kids' chopsticks that looked like large plastic tweezers. Then, as I was trying to salvage a little dignity, I choked on a soya bean. As my eyes bulged in my head, I noticed my date was smirking, so I started laughing too. It appeared my appalling eating habits were actually charming him!

He told me afterwards that he liked 'happy, slightly goofy people'. I'm sure there was a compliment in there somewhere. But it also shows that being a little nervous or haphazard can actually make you endearing.

You've probably heard it a thousand times before, but the other person is likely to be nervous too. If you can reassure yourself with that, all you really need to worry about are three things – smiling, asking questions and eye-contact. With these three in your arsenal, then you'll already be ahead of the game. Smiling instantly makes you seem approachable and friendly, which will put the other person at ease. Then, by asking him questions and holding his gaze, you are giving off a message that you are interested in what he has to say and not obsessed with talking about yourself – a big thing guys often complain girls do. And after a stiff drink and ten minutes of chatting, you'll probably find all that comes naturally anyway. So what are you waiting for?

How to meet men when you're shy

- Flirting nine to five. One of the best places to meet men is at work. You have to converse with them for your job, which gives you the perfect opportunity to flirt and invite them for a de-stress post-work drink.

- When you get to a certain age, it's obvious that you can no longer rely on nightclubs to net hot men (if you ever could), but there are heaps of social events that offer an opportunity to meet nice single men. Friends' weddings and birthdays are a gold mine – hell, I even pulled at my godmother's fiftieth!

- Friends of friends are another untapped dating pool. Everyone knows someone who's single, despite all evidence that they shouldn't be. So the next time your friend mentions a fittie who just shouldn't be on the market, demand to be introduced.

If you have succeeded in securing an introduction to a friend's ridiculously good-looking pal, then group nights out are always a safe bet. That way, if he does turn out to be a barbaric munter, you can politely lose him – as Hannah was forced to do with her blind date.

'When I was at college, my friend Elspeth had a host of hunky male friends,' she declares. 'We're talking proper Brad Pitt hotties, so when she declared that one of her male friends, Fred, had spied me and liked what he saw, I had high expectations.'

The following week, it was arranged that a group of Hannah and Elspeth's friends would head to a local nightclub where the mystery man would be introduced. Then, on the night of the big introduction, Hannah found herself waiting with excited anticipation outside the club.

'As we stood there, Elspeth announced she'd just seen him go past in a taxi,' Hannah recalls. 'Nervously, I scanned a group of lads walking across the road. This was at a time when nightclubs often had a strict dress code of jacket and tie, so I was looking for a hunky guy in a smart suit. But then my eyes fell on one chap in particular, and I just knew this was my mystery man.

'No, Fred wasn't a Brad Pitt lookalike. He wasn't even a Brendan Fraser in *The Mummy*. Worse still, he was very geeky, very short and wearing a nasty red suit – where on earth could you even get one of those, let alone go out and buy one on purpose?'

And as Bright Red Fred approached, Hannah 's horror grew tenfold. 'I spotted that he was wearing a jungle-scene tie complete with Mickey Mouse in an explorer hat,' she convulses. 'And grey slip-on shoes – with tassles!'

But seeing as this strange creature was a friend of Elspeth, Hannah didn't want to appear rude. After all, you shouldn't judge a book by its cover, should you? Perhaps he would turn out to be a riot – the most amusing man she'd ever met?

'As we stepped inside the nightclub, I had to give it to the other girls,' Hannah adds. 'They hid their smirks well.' But any hope that Fred would make up for his appalling dress sense with his sparkling wit soon faded. 'He was completely obnoxious,' reveals Hannah. 'As the night wore on, he became drunker and drunker and actually began insulting us all. By the time we piled in a taxi to go home, I wanted to strangle him – with his sodding Mickey Mouse tie!'

* * *

In another disastrous set-up, Greta reveals how her blind date became the stuff of nightmares.

It all began when her friends Melinda and Jasper decided she was the perfect match for their mate Colin. 'After being bamboozled for some time about how gorgeous he was, I agreed to meet him,' she divulges. 'So it was decided that the four of us would go to the Notting Hill Carnival together.'

Greta duly met her friends in a local pub and was immediately thrilled by their clever matchmaking. 'Colin was indeed gorgeous,' she says. 'He was also funny and nice and we got on like a house on fire.'

So after a lovely day out, everyone traipsed back to Melinda and Jasper's flat, and none too subtly they left Greta and Colin together to, er, get to know each other a bit better. They did indeed get on well, in fact so well that it wasn't long before they were coupled up in bed, ready for some action. But suddenly, Colin started to cry. 'Really loud, snotty sobs,' relates Greta. 'When I asked him what was wrong, he finally admitted that he had a long-term girlfriend whom he loved and wouldn't want to hurt!

'He told me that Melinda and Jasper couldn't stand his girlfriend and had instigated the meeting with the hope that he would instantly fall in love with me and break up with her!

'As I listened, incredulous, he added that as much as he thought I was really nice, he just couldn't do it,' Greta adds. 'So he got dressed and went back home to his girlfriend.

'I didn't know who I was more angry with: him for being so weak-willed or my supposed friends Melinda and Jasper for deliberately pushing me into such a horrible scenario.'

After those two disasters, I think it's only fitting that we end with a blind-date story guaranteed to warm the cockles.

Lisa was still reeling from some very discourteous treatment by her ex when she confided to her friend that she had one desire for the future – to find a hairy Geordie to love.

'Ah,' said her friend, 'I know one of those!'

And thus the arrangement was made that they would be introduced at her friend's birthday party in six weeks' time.

'I didn't really think about it much,' reveals Lisa. 'But when I saw her at the party and I asked where he was, she took me over to be introduced to him. Apparently, she'd already emailed him to say she had a big-boobed friend who wanted to get off with a Geordie – which was slightly embarrassing – but I went with it nonetheless.'

As it happens, Lisa was pleased with what she saw and cited The Geordie as very handsome. 'He looked like Jesus from the back and I remember telling another friend that I was going to try and pull The Messiah.' Later at the bar, Lisa, a routinely shy individual, decided to seize the moment.

'I bought my hairy Geordie a drink, we chatted for ages and ended up drunkenly snogging on a sofa. We had our first date a week later, fell totally in love, and I often think we might never have met if I hadn't had that conversation with my friend. Although he's not actually a Geordie at all, just Northern!'

So with that success story to cheer us up, let's move swiftly to speed dating. In theory, this is a great idea – three minutes to suss out if you like the look of them before they move on – loads of potential for love, surely? Well, not according to Lara.

'I was persuaded to go along to speed dating with my friend, but when we arrived, there were loads more women than men, so it wasn't a great start. I'm quite shy and the thought of meeting fifteen complete strangers was very daunting. I downed a bit of Dutch courage, then a bit more for good measure. Suffice it to say, by the end of the night I wasn't exactly wooing men with my sparkling wit. However, regardless of the alcohol, the night was just too much pressure for me.

'You might be able to tell whether you're attracted to someone in three minutes but that's about it. After that it's pure guesswork, and as far as I'm concerned, definitely not the way to meet people.'

So is it easier to suss out a potential suitor by scrolling through all their facts and stats online? You'd like to think so, but there's also no denying that the World Wide Web is a breeding ground for some absolute mentalists . . .

World Wide Web – a brief introduction to the Internut

'I've done a lot of Internet dating and I've spoken to some real weirdos. A man who liked to dress up as a baby and a guy who wanted to marry me but seemed offended when I suggested that perhaps he might like to meet me first. Another man was quite put out that I agreed to go on a date with someone else after I spoke to him. "I asked first," he said, as though I was a deli counter. I had to explain that it wasn't a case of "take a ticket and wait your turn."'

'My friend signed me up to "My Single Friend" for a laugh, and I arranged to go on a date with this guy after talking to him on the phone. He seemed like a good laugh but then he took me to Wetherspoons, where he made me pay for my own chips. He actually handed me the money, saying, "Mine cost this much." If you can't pay a pound fifty for some chips, we have a problem. He texted and rang several times and I gutlessly ignored him. Then I started a new job and found he was temping there for two weeks. I spent the entire time avoiding him.'

'I'd just split up with my husband and was staying with my parents when I started experimenting with Internet dating. I met up with a nice man and we went out several times over the course of about three weeks. Then, one night, when my parents went away, I invited him back. We'd got as far as my bedroom when he burst into tears, then ran off to his car and drove away with me chasing after his car. I never heard from him again.'

But it ain't all bad. Internet dating is now so in vogue that there are plenty of gems out there too, as Sara discovered.

'There's no doubt I've had my fair share of disasters with dating,' she says. 'There was the man who turned out to have only one leg – a little bit of warning would have been nice! Then there was the memorable date when I arrived in all of my finery, only for a passing pigeon to poo on my head – good timing. I didn't hear from my date again.

'Of the men I met through the Internet dating sites, some seemed nice at first, only to prove themselves absolute idiots, and others were just time-wasters. But there are some good guys out there too. When I met Steve on a site, I knew straight away he was something special. We just hit it off, had the same sense of humour and when we met in person for the first time, it felt as though we were on exactly the same wavelength.

'We've been together almost a year now and are about to go on holiday together, so I'm hopeful things will continue to go well. I tell my friends to try the Internet now. You might have to sort through some wasters, but it could all be worth it in the end.'

So, excitement! You think you've found a good-un. But a few dates in, with the potential of overnight stays in the offing, this is where all sorts of extra planning arises, such as keeping a toothbrush in your handbag, getting waxed and arming yourself with half-decent underwear. After all, you don't want to end up like the friend who ventured out in her bobbly old granny bloomers.

'What are these funny, furry things?' the object of her affection questioned, as he grappled with her knickers, and she frantically tried to switch the light off.

An unexpected night at his has consequences, particularly when you consider The Walk of Shame the following day. Catching the bus home first thing in the morning in your gold lamé dress and stilettos is never pleasant, but it's even worse if you have to head off to work.

Paige was working as a temp when she went out on a school night, got lucky with a guy she'd been seeing, and headed home to his lair. But the next morning, all trace of wild abandon gone, she realised that not only was she going to be late for work but she also had no change of clothes.

'At the time I was temping at a posh law firm and all I had was the top I was wearing the night before and a pair of jeans,' she says. 'Knowing I'd be late for work if I went home, I had to borrow a pair of his suit trousers and a belt. I then had to wear this strange combo to work with my high heels and top from the night before. I think everyone knew exactly what was going on!'

Unquestionably, the thing of utmost importance to consider is your own safety. You should avoid going home with a guy until you are sure that he's OK. Even if you think you've got him sussed, it pays to be on your guard, as Holly learnt the hard way.

'I started dating this crazy Danish guy who was five years younger than me, but I later discovered he was a complete operator, scamming his way around London,' she says. 'I ended it abruptly after I was burgled. I'd stupidly lent him my keys, as he needed somewhere to stay and my flatmate was abroad. Despite the fact that my flatmate's room was at the front, only my stuff was nicked. It was all very strange.'

So moving on, it's time to address the million-dollar question: what do men *really* make of a red-blooded female who sleeps with them on a first date?

While you would think that only the old-fashioned chaps would prefer to romance a lady who takes her time, it seems modern man can also view it as a red flag – but not necessarily a deal breaker. As one guy reveals, 'I'd like a bit more mystery; it's a marathon, not a sprint!'

Indeed, rather annoyingly, in a perfect show of double standards, it seems some men will judge you but feel smug about their own prowess. One lad announced, 'I know this is sexist and unfair, but I tend to think, yes, I'm a bad man and she's a slag. However, as a man I need to appreciate the fact that I must have been so utterly irresistible and pleasing that I quite literally charmed her pants off!'

Another announced, 'I'd think it was great if she did it because she liked sex and fancied me. I'd run a mile if I thought she was doing it because she thought she had to, or because she was a psycho.'

But if you do sleep with him on the first date and then have regrets, you shouldn't beat yourself up about it. As a nice young chap puts it, 'If the date was amazing, then it really wouldn't matter either way. And remember, almost everyone knows a married couple who slept together on the first date. If he really likes you, he's going to be into you regardless of whether you sleep with him or not.'

Sometimes, there's no need to endure dates with strangers or the politics of when to have sex. The great thing about being unattached is that you can now pull all those fit, single men with whom you've always shared a simmering sexual frisson.

For years, it's never quite happened – you were in a relationship, then he was, then you both were – but now you are free agents. Hurrah! So have a glance through your phone contacts book and see what treasures you can unearth. After all, a recent study suggested that one in three of us already has the number of our future soulmate stored in our phone. And, hell, if he isn't your soulmate, then it might be just as much fun finding out.

When Helen was reeling from a particularly painful break-up, a rendezvous with a hot man turned out to be the perfect remedy.

'I really fancied this guy I knew called Tristan,' she reveals. 'But we were never single at the same time. However, when I broke up with my boyfriend, it turned out he was a free agent too. We met up and he poured attention on me. Having such a gorgeous guy lusting after me did wonders for my shattered ego and we fell into bed. I was definitely more forward with him because I knew we already had chemistry and it really helped me to feel like a sex kitten again.'

So it went well for Helen, but what if you're apprehensive?

Sleeping with someone new can be a very daunting prospect, but sometimes you just need to get back in the saddle – as Bridget discovered.

'The first time I slept with a different guy I felt rubbish,' she admits, 'mainly because I was drunk and the man was unsuitable. But then I told myself it shouldn't be a big deal and I shouldn't give myself a hard time. So, a few weeks later, this time feeling more like Carrie Bradshaw, I actually met someone I liked and we ended up heading home together. Despite telling myself I could do the whole casual sex thing, once again I found it freaked me out, and confessed as much.'

Coincidentally, her companion revealed that he, too, was feeling rather raw about a failed relationship and with the barriers down they both relaxed. 'We spent the night in bed with no clothes on,' adds Bridget. 'We were both heart-broken, pouring over each other's text messages and confiding our deepest fears about why our relationships had floundered. When I admitted that I was worried a certain technique of mine wasn't up to scratch, he kindly offered that I could try my method out on him and he'd mark me out of ten.'

Turns out Bridget ranked in his top two ever. What a selfless guy!

Undoubtedly, while some of us battle with our inner prude, there are also many empowered single ladies who can enjoy a casual relationship with ease.

In many ways it has its advantages. If you're both consenting adults and in the mood, you don't even have to bother with the niceties of dinner and small talk. A scenario that suited Jenna perfectly . . .

'When I first moved to Leeds, I'd just come out of a two-year relationship and didn't want anything serious,' she explains. 'Plus my job working as a barmaid in a trendy bar ensured I had plenty of dates. I was going out, pulling loads of people and having a great time. But one night a really hunky six-foot guy came to the bar and proceeded to buy pink Bacardi Breezers for himself and his mates.

'I've always been a bit cheeky, so I immediately started berating him for being a big girl.' It turned out the 'big girl' was a South African called Damian who was living in Manchester, and despite Jenna's teasing, he had taken quite a shine to her.

'After we had talked for a little bit, he asked for my number. I wouldn't give it to him at first, but then he promised to take me out to dinner the next time he was in Leeds.'

Sure enough, two weeks later, Damian called and took Jenna to dinner. And it went so well that they continued the party back at her flat. 'He ended up staying for two days!' she laughs. 'Then after that, I'd see him whenever he was in Leeds.'

For the next twelve months, Jenna and Damian continued to see each other on and off, but it was always very relaxed. 'It was just really nice to have such a stress-free, no-strings arrangement,' she says. 'We'd go out, have a great time, and then end up between the sheets. Then the next morning we'd lie in bed chatting and he'd test me on capital cities around the world. It was one of his talents and he knew every one!'

Predictably, after a while, Damian headed back to South Africa. 'We had one last no-strings night together,' reveals Jenna. 'Then we bid each other a fond farewell. I was a bit sad to see him go but we still email occasionally.'

The rule of attraction is a curious thing. Sometimes you can desire a man on sight, only to be bitterly disappointed by your first embrace. He's a nice guy, but when it's like kissing your brother? Ugh, no.

Fran had high hopes when she was set up with a friend of her flatmate, but was left so disappointed by their first snog that she practically had to fight him off.

'It was at the end of the date when he went in for the kiss,' she reveals. 'I kissed him back, but there was no chemistry at all. It felt like kissing a dummy. Yet he didn't seem to be getting this at all and started taking off his shirt. I immediately tried to stall him, saying I didn't want to rush into anything, but it took a long time for him to get the hint. Eventually, he announced that he'd sleep on the floor and he left at the crack of dawn the next day.' Ouch.

In another tale of failed chemistry, Zeta made the mistake of seducing a workmate. 'He was seven years older than me, but turned out to be completely inexperienced,' she says. 'At one point we were in bed and I had to move his hand about three centimetres.

'"Oh," he said, "So I wasn't far off then?"'

In a slightly more lusty, but decidedly alarming story, Kim describes her first post break-up tryst with a handsome sailor while visiting New Zealand. 'He looked like a cross between Ben Affleck and Orlando Bloom, so I was only too happy to have a bit of a dance, flirt and drink with him,' she says.

But while her ocean-faring hunk cleaned up in the looks department, his smooth dialogue was not up to scratch. 'The first warning sign should've come when he announced that he was off to "tinkle from the winkle", but before that he was going to kiss me,' reveals Kim. 'So the perfect sunset kiss was immediately ruined by thoughts of him peeing.'

Regardless, Kim put it behind her. They talked more, danced more, and she made it clear that she was in New Zealand to have fun and no more. 'To be honest, it had been a fair while since I'd seen a naked man and I just wanted a good shag,' she adds. 'So we went back to his, got naked and then he told me that he wanted "to make passionate love to me".'

Choosing to ignore this inappropriate turn of phrase, Kim carried on, until her bed pal started to whisper in her ear, 'Tell me you love me.' Slightly scared, Kim once again chose to ignore him, but her smitten sailor was not giving up that easily.

'When I pretended I hadn't heard, he looked me in the eyes and repeated, "Tell me you love me, I wanna hear you say those words." I did a classic hug and roll and made my excuses, but then he persuaded me to stay.'

Hours later, with all thoughts of love forgotten, Kim geared herself up for round two, which was to be an altogether different experience.

'This time, in the heat of the moment, he asked me, "So do you know how to really turn a man on?" Then just as I was wondering what exactly I was supposed to say, he answered for me: "Yeah, but it's illegal."

'What do you say to that? I got dressed, handed him a false phone number and legged it!'

So the hunt goes on.

But, be warned, for every good man you seek, you'll find a plethora of oddballs, social misfits or appalling dullards. My nutter radar seems to be permanently on high alert, but then I've always been far too polite for my own good.

I was always incapable of shaking off rubbish dates or the loser I'd been stuck talking to at the bar. It meant that hours of my life have been wasted listening to boring bastards harping on about their work profit margins, or arrogant arses telling me about their pompous attitudes to life, not to mention enduring the halitosis or shower of spittle projecting from someone who was rudely invading my body space.

Thankfully, a friend, Ruth, taught me to be more proactive. One night, we were in a bar in Birmingham when two men approached and offered to buy us drinks. As a rule, I will never accept a drink from a guy until I have sussed him out, as I hate that feeling that you are indebted to someone. I suspected this duo to be pretty smarmy, so I was just about to refuse, when Ruth cheekily pointed to the most expensive champagne cocktail on the list.

'We'll have that one,' she announced. 'But only if you have it too.'

As one of the unwitting men forked out in the region of

fifty pounds for four drinks, my heart plummeted. That's it, I thought. Now we'll be stuck talking to them all bloody night.

As predicted, they were not only smarmy, but also very tiresome. We were immediately paired off (I'm not sure whose wretched bore was worse) but they clearly thought their luck was in. After about thirty minutes of this hell, Ruth nudged me. 'We're just going to the loo,' she announced.

We'd been sat close to the main entrance, so had to walk towards the back of the bar to go up a winding staircase to the toilets. Halfway up the stairs Ruth turned to me. 'We're ditching them,' she said.

'But how?' I asked. 'If we leave, they'll see us; we've got to walk right past them.'

'I've got a plan,' she whispered.

So after we'd peed and preened, I followed Ruth along the corridor from the toilets past the winding staircase. Lo and behold, there was our escape route – a disabled lift that dropped you off right next to the exit of the bar.

Giggling, we sneaked in and pressed the ground floor button. But at the bottom I saw we had one last hurdle. We needed to sneak out a side door to the exit, and there was still a chance the bores might see us. Suddenly, I lost my bottle. 'We can't!' I exclaimed. 'They're going to rumble us!'

'We can!' Ruth urged me. 'They really won't.'

Then suddenly we received a rallying call from behind us. Unbeknown to us, a couple snogging in the entrance had overheard our plight.

'Come on, bab!' the man whooped in a thick Brummie accent. 'Be strong. The force is with you!'

And with that, Ruth pushed my bum out the door and we scuttled out into the night without looking back. Sadly, my umbrella was cruelly discarded that night, but it was a small price to pay for our freedom.

In a comical twist, about four weeks later, Ruth was in a yoga class at our local gym, when who should she see glaring at her from across the room? It was one of the bores, now looking decidedly more angry than smug. He clearly recognised her and was not at all impressed.

It was the only yoga class she attended where she actually left feeling much more tense. Naturally, it was the least we deserved after leading those lads on such a costly and pointless mission.

In another story of a perfect come-uppance, Tina reveals how she was caught out ditching a date at university.

'I worked behind the bar at a student union that was frequented by rugby boys who thought they were really cool. But when I got asked out by a really fit one, I duly accepted. He wanted to take me to this really swish oyster bar for dinner, followed by theatre, so I bought a new outfit and shoes and was really excited.

'When we met, we sat down and he started to talk. Not only did he have the worst breath, but he was also SO BORING. He had nothing to say about anything. I was doing an English degree and was in that precious first flush of thinking I was a genius because I was reading six books a week, when he declared with gusto that "reading was for people with too much time on their hands and no original ideas of their own", before going back to talking about rugby. Again.

'We ordered our starters and mains, and I just felt this mist descend. I had to get out. So I said I was just popping to the loo, grabbed my coat on the way, put the lid down, took my shoes off and jumped (the window wasn't high). I then got a cab back to the student bar, where I agreed to fill in for half an hour for a girl off sick. Fifteen minutes in, someone tapped my arm and said, "Mine's a pint." It was him. I was mortified.'

Maybe the best bet is to be a bit more upfront about your intentions. In fact, I'll never forget the time my friend and I were expertly ditched by two Scottish rugby players during a night out in Bath.

They'd lost against the home side that day and, after buying us drinks, they clearly sensed our disinterest, so downed their pints and walked off. I guess they weren't about to admit defeat for the second time in one day and it was a smooth, unashamed operation.

I think the main issue is having the guts to 'not give a stuff' if someone else thinks you are rude or impolite. But if they're a stranger, why should you care?

As Elise confides, 'I once felt compelled to behave badly on a date as it became clear that the guy was just trying to use me to get football tickets. My dad was on the board of a big football club and I agreed to the date under the illusion that he might actually be interested in me. But, no, he clearly had another agenda.

'He struck me as a bit of a prude, but halfway thorough the second course, it became apparent that his fascination was not with me, but my father's job. He came right out with it, asking if I could get him and his mates some tickets to a big game.'

Livid to have discovered his ungentlemanly agenda, Elise was tempted to leave, but she decided to finish her food and launched into a charmless offensive to put him in his place.

'I was so annoyed that I basically got hammered and did everything I could think of to annoy him,' she admits. 'Then, because he wasn't impressed with how much I was drinking, I necked even more and embarked on completely crass topics of conversation. I said I'd been out with loads of blokes and made up a story about having a threesome. It seemed he was a prude and it had the right result.

'He still insisted on doing the right thing by dropping me at my door, but left me with a brisk goodnight. He didn't get his footy tickets and we never saw each other again!'

Dates from hell: the romances that were over almost as soon as they began

'One time, a bus driver randomly asked me out. I admired his courage so I agreed. I thought it would make a great "guess how we met" story for our grandchildren. But when we met up in a horrible bar in Manchester, I had the most excruciating hour of my life. He started by asking odd questions, like, "Do you think you're infertile?", with no preamble or appropriate context. Then a couple minutes later, he asked, "Have you ever been out with a black man?" We were sitting between the exit and the ladies' toilets, so I couldn't even sneak out. It was horrible. I didn't return his calls.'

'When I went out with a guy who couldn't make any of his own decisions, I wasn't impressed. I had to choose where we met, the date and time and even suggest what he had to drink. He told me he was changing his hair because his mother told him to and was on a diet because his mother thought he should lose some weight. He also lived in university halls, which according to him was "brilliant" because you didn't have to clean or pay bills. He was thirty-two.'

'On our first date, I got so drunk I was sick, and spent the night snogging the poor guy with my beer goggles firmly intact. When I met him for the second date, I totally didn't fancy him, so spent the whole time avoiding his advances. I think he thought I was a total freak.'

'I once went on a date with a more mature gentleman. He took me to a Chinese restaurant and it was all going well until it came to paying for the bill. He insisted on paying for it all, got his card out, but couldn't remember his pin. Again he wouldn't let me pay and said he was going home to get the number. I was left sitting awkwardly in the restaurant for half an hour. He did come back and pay, but I didn't see him again.'

'When I eventually got the date I had been waiting for with an extremely handsome officer, it was ruined by a repeat of the Chinese takeaway I'd had the night before. I spent the whole time running to the loo, and if that wasn't bad enough, when I got home and proceeded to tell my flatmates all about it, I heard a knock at the door. I had left my hat in his car and he had been on the doorstep listening to everything. I never heard from him again.'

And, finally, from the men . . .

'I once made the mistake of turning up for a date a bit drunk. As a result, I was being over-chatty and bizarrely acting quite camp. I could see in her eyes that this wasn't going to get me anywhere. After a couple of drinks she told me she was heading home, and although I offered to walk with her, she declined and in fact walked *me* to a bus stop. It was quite a while before my bus came and then, as it drove past a pub, I saw her outside drinking and laughing with some men. It was not the most reassuring moment, nor did it do much for irresistible sex god status.'

'I remember trying to impress a particularly hot blonde on a first date by chasing a bag thief through Covent Garden. I would have been a hero but said thief threw the bag at me while I was at full speed, causing me to trip up, dislocate my shoulder and break a thumb. I spent the rest of the first date in hospital. On my own.'

'I once became so drunk on a date that I fell asleep in the girl's car on the way home. I was so comatose that when she arrived back at mine, she couldn't wake me and ended up just pushing me out of the vehicle. I woke up some minutes later on my drive, dazed and confused. We did not have a second date.'

So, how do you ditch that bad first date?

Planning, planning and more planning. This is the key to any successful escape. The inner romantic in all of us always considers whether this is the date that might lead to love, but there's always a good chance he'll be yet another frog you have to kiss (or not) along the way.

* * *

Any sensible dater knows that you need to go into a date with an escape plan.

1. Make sure your first date isn't something that has to last a long time. A three-course dinner isn't as easy to get away from as a coffee or a few drinks.

2. If he's a groper (and believe me there's no reason for his hand to be firmly attached to your bottom half an hour after meeting), then he's plainly a lech, so don't even bother being polite. A disgusted look, a huff, quick goodbye and swift exit is called for.

3. Always have a friend on stand-by – this is good advice for your own safety but also lets them rescue you if he turns out to be an oddball. Get them to send you a text or call around forty-five minutes into the date (much longer and you'll realise how long an hour really can be). If you're having fun, then a quick OK will be fine. If not, then that dire emergency – your house has been broken into, your car stolen or your best friend is having an emotional crisis – will help you make a quick exit.

4. He's probably going to guess that you're lying anyway, but if you want to try to save face, a sudden onset of a migraine or similar illness will do the trick. Anything more dramatic and you could land yourself in a sticky situation, as Carla did. It was during a dreary film at the cinema, as her date tried to stick his tongue down her ear, that Carla had the bright idea of feigning appendicitis – a bit extreme but it gives you some idea of how gross he was.

But instead of letting her go to hospital on her own (despite her insistence), not only did her date drive her there, but he also walked her into A & E shouting 'my girlfriend has suspected appendicitis' at the top of his voice. To make matters worse, he announced that his best friend was working at the hospital and immediately called him.

Carla was sharply shoved into a wheelchair, rushed through with gold-star treatment, only to be walked out again thirty minutes later as his doctor friend told her date through clenched teeth, 'She's not worth it, mate.'

5. But is honesty ever the best policy? So you get there and the picture you saw on the Internet dating site must have been taken at least ten years and fifty burgers ago. While you might want to recoil in horror and run as fast as your legs will carry you, there's no need to be mean. He's probably been on just as many bad dates as you have, and nobody needs to have their confidence shattered by an outright rejection or by being stood up. Sit down, have a drink and a chat for a while and, if you're brave enough, simply tell him it was very nice to meet him but you don't think you'd be quite right together and leave. You'll feel all grown up and everything.

Of course, what you really need is a Harry Potter-style invisibility cloak or a partner in crime to lead you to a secret hidden exit as found in the posh restaurants and clubs for drunken celebrities who want to avoid the paparazzi. Once during a holiday to America, I went to an odd little bar in Milwaukee. Upon arrival my companion and I were told we had to pass an initiation test before we could enter. Bemused and a bit pissed, we agreed.

We were then given pom-poms and blonde schoolgirl plaits and were made to jump around chanting like cheerleaders before we could set foot inside. As we stepped into the bar, there was a big cheer and laughing. The joke was on us – a hidden camera had broadcast our antics to the whole bar. After I'd recovered from my humiliation, I was informed by a fun lady from the local tourist board that this very venue was Milwaukee's top spot to ditch a date.

'All you do,' she told me, beckoning me towards a telephone box in an annex of the bar, 'is tell them you just need to make a call. Then you come in here, dial a special number and hey presto!'

With that, like a scene from *Batman*, a secret door magically creaked open and a long corridor led us out on to the streets below. Brilliant!

8.

The boys have their say

So we've heard what it's like from the girls' point of view, but it would only be fair to give the guys a break, wouldn't it?

What is it really like for them from the first moment of attraction to the point where it all goes tits up and they find themselves tossed back on to the single's market? How does it feel when a cruel femme fatale mercilessly dumps them? And what's the real explanation behind their most reckless and heartbreaking behaviour?

You'll be pleased to know that I have managed to persuade a panel of charming (cough) young men to lift the lid on how men really think. This lovely (but at times not so nice to date) bunch of willing males have personally traced their own relationship successes and failures for your benefit. So, after some relentless man bashing, fasten your seatbelts. It's time for the boys to have their say about the dating game.

The course of true love never did run smooth, so William Shakespeare once said, and while we like to kid ourselves that all men are unfeeling dirtbags, it is true that they suffer their ups and downs in the dating world too.

In fact, our first willing participant, Declan, maintains that the habitually humiliating experiences he endured from trying to secure his very first date through to university and beyond, ensured he soon grasped the rules that shaped his dating habits into adulthood.

'Like many men, I learnt the universal truth "treat 'em mean, keep 'em keen" the hard way, following several years of being trampled on by the unfair sex,' he retorts. 'Do you have any idea what you evil teenage girls put boys like me through?

'I can remember only too well the abject terror I used to experience whenever I tried to talk to girls during my adolescent years. It was like the final frontier in becoming a proper teenager – you had your mates, you had your bike, but you just couldn't quite get the courage together to talk to girls. You were just so mean!'

To his dismay, as Declan attempted to woo pretty young ladies, he found himself being rebuffed with ferocious abandon – girls would turn their back on him, laugh in his face and run off.

'I'm sure I gave it my best shot,' he says. 'When I saw the girl I liked standing there with all her mates in a group, I would summon up all my courage and willpower to go over and break the silent bond that separated our tribes.'

But sadly, he confides, the conversation with the cute freckled girl often went like this:

Declan: 'Erm, hi!'

Freckled girl (sounding bored): 'Yeah?'

Declan: 'Well, I was just wondering . . .'

Freckled girl: 'Wait a minute (slight splutter). Are you asking me out?'

Declan (his face growing redder by the minute): 'Well, erm, yes?'

Freckled girl (guffawing loudly): 'Ha ha! Oh my gosh! I can't believe you just done that, I am going to have to . . . hang on . . . MICHELLE!!!!!!'

Cue the object of Declan's affection running off to whisper in her mate's ear, before the pair of them erupt into riotous laughter. All at his expense.

'For the record, this happened frequently throughout my school years,' Declan says. 'Girl after girl, who I thought perhaps might be interested, just wasn't. Terrified of rejection, I'd try approaching the girl's best friend.

'"Can you ask your mate out for me," I'd ask tentatively.

'"I did and she said NO," would come the blunt response.'

Of course, this was all back in the day before mobiles, so if Declan wanted to bypass the hysterical pack of screeching girl mates, he would actually have to ring the young lady's landline and speak to a proper adult.

'It was always the same scenario,' he reveals. 'Her mother would answer, instantly causing me to quake in my boots, and I'd politely explain that I was in Jenny's class and would like to speak to her.

'Next, filtering down the line I'd hear a muffled exchange between mother and daughter, possibly in the kitchen, with both of them clearly trying to keep their voices down. My heart would beat faster as I waited, then I'd start to hear footsteps coming along the parquet floor-ing towards the phone. What is she thinking? I'd wonder. Should I have done this?

'Then, Jenny's voice would confirm all my doubts in an instant with a sulky hello. A glutton for punishment, I'd still ask her to the cinema, only for her to hit me with a big, fat, in-your-face rejection.'

It was these experiences as a gangly teenager that Declan claims caused him to wonder if his courting attempts were deeply flawed. 'I began to think that perhaps girls can just smell how desperate you are,' he says.

After one rejection too many, Declan then began to grasp that perhaps the way forward was to treat them with the same weary disdain. As he got older, he realised that nothing really changes, except perhaps the manner in which boys approach the girls and the manner in which they are rebuffed or dumped.

'The rules of attraction that were formed in the playground are just dressed up a bit as you enter adulthood,' he suggests. 'So after years of trying unsuccessfully to ask girls out, I realised that I was giving out the wrong vibes. So eager was I to curry favour with the object of my desire, I ended up looking like I was desperate and slightly, well, weird.

'Then I finally cracked the conundrum. I worked out that as soon as I stopped giving a shit, girls were much easier to come by.'

Maybe it was a case of Declan giving the impression he was a lot more fun or interesting or dangerous. Or perhaps he just managed to exhibit himself as a better all-round proposition by being almost challenging to girls and turning the tables on the situation. But either way, being a tad standoffish and deciding not to jump through hoops worked.

'Women, I found, reacted very differently to a persona that suggests you are perhaps more contented and confident in yourself than you actually are,' he reveals. 'When I attempted to snare a girl, the less interested I seemed, the more interested she was.'

So next time you see a gaggle of evil little schoolgirls sniggering and ridiculing some poor lovestruck little wretch on a bus, you will know this is the point that turns good boys bad. Don't approach them, though, you might get arrested – or even worse, mugged for your mobile phone.

So, at last, an explanation as to why men like to keep us guessing and on our toes. It's a defence mechanism to stop us from humiliating them in the dating playground. But that doesn't mean they never suffer. Even when all their defences are in place, they still get shot down in the cruellest ways imaginable . . .

'My first love broke up with me and became a lesbian,' reveals an unlucky young man called Shaun. 'Neither of us had been with anyone before and our relationship lasted for two years. But when we split up, she immediately started dating a girl called Lauren.

'Previously Lauren stayed over at her house a lot. I just thought they were close friends but it turns out they were lovers!

'In hindsight, for her to sleep with a girl wasn't so surprising. She was adventurous in bed and enjoyed trying new things, so having a same-sex relationship was perhaps the logical progression. She openly had a crush on Drew

Barrymore and had a nude poster of her on her bedroom wall. I should have seen the signs!

'I found out when I was trying to make plans for Valentine's day. She kept being evasive and wouldn't commit to anything. Eventually, she confessed that she wanted to spend the day with Lauren and that was when our relationship ended.

'The penny dropped when I saw them snogging at a gig a couple of weeks later. I spent an hour bawling on my friend's shoulder.

'Up until the point she broke my heart, I'd always thought that if it did end, it would be me ending it, which was terribly arrogant of me. I was distraught when it happened and had lots of silly one-night-stands to make myself feel better. But things picked up after about nine months when I went to uni and found a girlfriend there. Hooray!

'I heard Lauren left her lesbian days behind after about a year and is now married with a baby, so I guess it was an experimental phase.'

So next time you find yourself on the receiving end of bad treatment from a bloke, just give him a little bit of benefit of the doubt – he might have been to hell and back too.

As one man says: 'As far as falling in love goes, I believe women fall easier, while men fall harder. Men have a tremendous amount of trouble dealing with the amount of vulnerability that love opens you up to, as well as recovering from it.'

Indeed, while being cruelly dumped hurts for both sexes,

men appear to suffer more when it comes to having their pride wounded. It's like they think they've failed in some way. There are concerns that their mates might judge them or rib them, and the last thing they want is to lose face in front of the boys.

If they have fallen for a girl who then tramples on them, they might appear fine, but deep down it could take them quite some time to recover, as Wes reveals . . .

'On my third day of university, I saw a girl walk by and immediately thought "She's The One. That girl is cool." I walked over and started speaking with her. Her name was Lana, and we ended up together for all three years of university. We were inseparable, best friends (we even exchanged email passwords), and after graduation, agreed we would stay close but sort of pursue our own paths for a bit.

'I went to live in Budapest, and she went to work in the north of England. Her emails, though, started drying up as the lonely Budapest winter descended. I went back home for Christmas and sent her a present, as I always did, hoping against hope that I'd hear back from her.'

But two days after Christmas, Wes received grim news.

'Lana called me and, although I don't remember the exact details of the conversation, she was irrationally angry,' he reveals. 'She told me she hated me and that she was living with another guy.

'I was utterly dumbfounded by this, and spent about a month or so back in Budapest licking my wounds before I remembered that I knew her email password. "Fuck it," I decided, "I'm going to see what's been going on." Maybe this whole other guy business was just something she made up to twist the knife. But that's how I found out they'd got married.'

Remarkably, Wes was eventually able to forgive Lana. 'Much later she explained that generating anger towards me was sort of her way to burn through all the feelings that she still had,' he adds. 'She did it to distance herself from me and get over everything. But even with that explanation it still broke my heart.'

Whether people lash out at the end of relationships to make themselves feel better or just say something without realising how deep it will cut you, most of the time if they're treating you badly, it's about them – not you.

Distance had obviously taken its toll on Wes's relationship but, although he didn't see it, was it really that unexpected?

First and foremost, men don't like change – they'll happily sit and let relationships rumble along, not thinking that the girl might not be seeing it quite the same way. So, while Wes was in Budapest kidding himself that everything was fine and he'd be able to pick up his relationship, Lana was moving on.

But that's the thing about blokes, they can be their own worst enemies. While girls like to plan, to finalise things, to instinctively nest and get everything in order, men admit they are happier to go with the flow. They like to procrastinate, to deal with things when it's absolutely necessary, and not before – which leads to mix-ups and misunderstandings between the two sexes, as Mike found.

'The worst thing a girl did to me was sleep with my best

friend when I was overseas,' he says. 'Before I left, I told the girl I'd been dating that she couldn't sleep with certain guys, like Terry or Chris – but aside from that she was free to do what she liked, and that, who knows, maybe in the future we could get back together again.

'She then went and slept with my best friend Rick, but I only found out when she moved to New York, where I was, a year later. When I asked her why she had to go and sleep with Rick, she cheekily said that I didn't mention Rick as one of the people that she couldn't sleep with. So I let my pride prevent me from getting back with her.'

OK, so I know what you're thinking: he went ABROAD. HE broke up with her, he left her with an order not to go near certain friends, and then when she didn't actually break his 'rule', he still refused to go out with her again. I can hear your collective sigh of relief at her lucky escape.

But, to be fair, it's no wonder he felt slighted. The girl who he had a soppy dream of being reunited with had gone against the one thing he'd asked her not to do if there was to be any hope of them getting back together. She also committed the cardinal sin of pulling his friend. The vast majority of men view their mate's exes as an absolute no-go, so he felt he'd been slighted on both sides.

When she pulled his friend, she must have known the repercussions. Perhaps she was even trying to make him jealous or teach him a lesson for not making a proper commitment to her? But for him, pride won and scuppered any chance they might have had.

Indeed, pride seeps out of men like testosterone. They don't want to be shown up, made to feel bad or stupid and so, at the first hint that any of those things could happen, they run, hide their feelings, and drink and chase skirt to get over it. And, well, considering the way some of us behave, it's not really surprising.

The worst thing a girl ever did to me was ...

'Dump me for her ex.'

'Break up with me over my reluctance to settle down and then set her bloody dog on me! The little sod chased me down the street.'

'Get her dad to change the locks while I was out.'

'String me along for a whole summer, giving me the impression I was in with a chance, when all she really wanted was a bit of drama. That harridan stole the summer of '96 from me!'

'Tell my friends that I'd forced myself on her, then seduce me when I had a new girlfriend.'

'Cheat on me when she went on holiday. I was away, too, but missed her so much I wanted to come home early. The day I got back, I went round to hers and she said it was over. I cried and begged her to stay

> with me. Then I found out she'd slept with someone else.'
>
> 'After five years of an on-off, long-distance relationship and six weeks after deciding we'd finally be together – after I'd quit my job, bought my plane ticket and a ring – she told me that she wanted to get back with a guy she'd been seeing four months earlier. Apparently, he was more "in touch" with who she was now rather than in love with a snapshot of who she'd been five years ago. Maybe she was right.'

Pretty harsh, eh? And proof that break-ups are just as painful to go through when you're a man. Men certainly feel the pain and then some – but often feel they are forced to pretend they're big and hairy enough to cope.

As one lad eloquently sums it up: 'To think that we don't feel it too is tosh. We just have a greater capacity for alcohol.'

That happens to be the bitter reality for Martin, still smarting after an older woman chewed him up and spat him out. 'I'll never forget the pain I went through when Lianne dumped me,' he says. 'She was a single mum and I met her on a blind date. After just ten minutes she asked if I had two pound coins on me. I asked why and she said to buy some condoms as I was going home with her that night!

'She was amazing in the bedroom department, but was

also very bright and great fun. She had two kids who I loved, and while it started out as just a lust-fuelled fling, within a few months it had become serious.'

But then, one day, Lianne uttered the most hurtful words a man can hear: 'You're just too nice for me.'

'She didn't mince her words when she wanted to end it,' Martin reckons. 'She denied anyone else was involved, but I later found out she was back with her ex. I was devastated and it took me weeks to get over it.'

So the sentence 'you're too nice for me' is a killer, isn't it? I hope you'll join me in hanging your head in collective shame. So many of us have used that line, we've all thought it and then when the next man is desperately mean we just can't understand what drove him to it.

Yet if girl after girl reprimands a bloke for being 'too nice', it's no wonder he often proceeds with aloof caution when it comes to matters of the heart.

Explaining why he became once bitten twice shy, Cameron says, 'I had my heart broken twice, all before the age of twenty-one, when I was quite sensitive and naive. I got a lot harder-hearted after that.'

And that's what men admit they do. If they've come a cropper in the past they build barriers and replace naive optimism with suspicious cynicism. As another guy reveals: 'We control our feelings carefully before we fall and then if the shit does hit the fan, we put on our best Dalek disguises. All you can see is the hard body armour, but underneath there is actually a jibbering mutant trying his best not to fall to pieces.'

* * *

So let's get to the nitty gritty – the stuff we all want to know – how chaps deal with the pain and make it look so easy? Well, put it this way, there are A LOT of smoke and mirrors involved . . .

Boy's don't cry – how we get over you

'It's all positive mental attitude and pretending to your mates that you're fine – blokes don't really encourage moping.'

'I get over a break-up by lying that I couldn't care less and then weeping at home alone.'

'There's nothing quite like pulling a new girl to help you to get over an old one. I guess there comes a need to reassure yourself that you are indeed attractive and wonderful, and there are plenty of girls out there just waiting for someone like you to come along.'

'I deal with the pain by going out drinking with mates and enjoying being single.'

'We don't relish the drama as much as girls do. We still hurt, but we try to keep a lid on it.'

'I get over a girl by falling in love with another. Unfortunately, it sometimes takes a long time.'

'I like to take time out of the game and go through a revamp. I detox, get back to the gym, spend time and money on myself. I suppose it's a bit of self-ego-massage.'

'You just have to change how you think about the girl. You can't allow any sentimentality. You have to move on.'

'The best way to get over heartache is by drinking, letting time pass and having meaningless sex with other women.'

'I get sad, then angry and tell myself she didn't deserve me – which obviously she didn't!'

'I cry and listen to Jeff Buckley, then I get drunk with my friends.'

'We focus on the positive side of being single – there are lots of women with breasts out there. Ha!'

So the last one was said in jest (well, kind of), but it just goes to show that boys also experience weeping, wrath and ruin – periods of time when they mope around listening to melancholy music and drinking far too much when the girl they love has left. But they also find a way to view it quite clinically and pragmatically by thinking positively and getting back out there.

But what about the ones who do bugger off without a thought for your welfare? The cads who call it off with the cool, blasé attitude of someone terminating their phone contract? What's that all about? Have you been dating a closet Vulcan? Did that small procedure for his in-growing toenail last month accidentally result in a lobotomy? Why did he end it so callously?

Turns out it could be a number of reasons. It might be immaturity or the fact a little sadistic part of him knows that not showing emotion winds you up a treat. It could also be because he's just too cowardly to tell you the truth behind why he wants to split.

Anyway, here's THEIR show-and-tell therapy . . .

She was completely ungracious

'My first real relationship was with a girl I met in a club,' says Scott. 'For a while she was attractive, fun and gregarious and I behaved impeccably. There was no game playing and on our first date I even met her parents, which was a real testament to my interest in her.

'Then a few months in, I travelled a long way to see her at university and she was very distant with me. All day she was curt and unresponsive, a little madam basically, which was somewhat of an oddity. After all, I had charmed the folks, kind of played it fair and made the effort at her behest to travel the distance to go and see her. On the way home she called me and bizarrely had a further go at me about some perceived insult or something that she believed I had done. This sealed the deal and I never returned another call nor made any attempt to remedy the situation.

'Around a year later, she called me up and left a message on my answer phone saying what a fool she'd been and that she really had made the worst mistake of her life. Quite odd, given her determination not to make an effort at the time.'

The reason he left

When I read a story like this a little part of me cringes in recognition. I can remember that time when I thought I was a little too big for my boots, when I assumed I had him right where I wanted him and that if I threw my weight around he'd totally take it. It's the old 'you're too nice' scenario all over again.

The fact is, Scott was nice but he wasn't a mug. He'd made a big effort, charmed her parents, travelled to see her, but clearly there wasn't enough mystique in him treating her so well. So his girlfriend got a bit cocky, wrongly assuming he was so into her that he'd take whatever she dished out. It all backfired and she lost out.

And we wonder why they treat us mean . . .

I suspected she was cheating on me

'When my girlfriend moved towns to be with me, I was concerned she didn't know many people,' Aiden says. 'So I did everything to make her happy and help her settle in. At first, she came out a lot with my friends, but after a while I sensed that she hated relying on my social circle. So, as she was a keen athlete, I suggested she join a local running club.

'This she did and it went very well; she got lots of new friends. But before long she seemed distracted and cold. I began to wonder if her head had been turned.

'I travelled quite a lot with work and one week I came home to find a framed picture of David Beckham hanging on our bedroom wall. My girlfriend was quite short, yet the picture was heavy and placed quite high on the wall. I immediately wondered who had helped her to put it up. My suspicion was further compounded by two champagne flutes left out on my kitchen table. She'd obviously been having a good time while I was away. Upon further snooping, I discovered that a good-looking male runner from her club had been checking his emails on our computer. There were also a few flirty texts to him on her mobile phone.

'When I confronted her about some of the things I'd found, she denied any wrongdoing. But I packed my bags and walked out anyway. We never spoke again.'

The reason he left

Again, a classic case of wounded male pride. Aiden had no concrete evidence that his girlfriend had cheated but he felt betrayed by her. After he acted kindly and encouraged her to pursue things to make her happy, she was far from gracious and had, at the very least, been flirting with someone else. Perhaps if they had discussed it properly, the relationship could have been saved, but when she refused to talk about it, he walked out without another word to spite her. He did it to get at her, but the sad reality is it hurt him more than she'd ever know.

We were a destructive influence on each other

Anthony's relationship with Kayleigh revolved largely around getting shit-faced. As is often the case with alcohol, their lairy sessions on the sauce could fuel hair-raising rows.

'We both did and said awful things,' he admits. 'On my part, I got very drunk at a family dinner and insulted her sister. Another time I turned up to a party of hers and spray-painted her wardrobe green. It turns out it was hundreds of years old and handed down the generations. When I look back, I think we both had a real drinking problem. The one good thing I did before I broke up with her was to talk her out of dancing at a strip club.

'When I ended it, I was quite cold and immediately cut off all contact so I could give up the booze. She was very upset and just couldn't understand why it was happening.'

The reason he left

Some people should just never be together. Whether you've both got a drink problem, have bad tempers or are just so laid back that you'll end up sleep-walking through life, being a destructive influence on each other leads to all manner of problems.

Breaking up is all about being selfish and Aiden felt he had to cut contact for his own good. It wasn't personal, he just knew that it was easy to fall back into a drinking habit – and having a partner in crime makes it too tempting.

She was too scared to love me

'I met my perfect girl at a point when she was emerging from two back-to-back relationships in which, as she put it, she seemed to have lost her sense of herself and her feeling of independence,' David says. 'We sort of fell into a relationship almost by accident, which was quickly sparkling and magical in so many ways. We both needed it at that point in our lives.

'We clicked, we harmonised – she said over and over that she'd never met someone who understood her so soulfully. But that, ironically, was our downfall. The closer she got to me and the more she felt the tug of love, the more fearful she became of losing herself or slipping away from that fragile sense of control. The closer we grew, the worse it got. She would go from being tender and loving to nasty and stand-offish in the blink of an eye. So, finally, I ended it, moved countries and took up with someone else.'

The reason he left

What a sad little tale. But clearly after trying his hardest to convince his girlfriend that it was OK to fall for him, David felt completely vulnerable. He felt his girlfriend was on a path to self-destruct, and although he tried to help, you can't always fix other people.

If they had stayed together he would have felt she was always one step from running away. A relationship lasting is down to the two people involved risking everything to allow themselves to fall one hundred per cent.

I was an immature jerk

'When I was seventeen, I dated the most beautiful girl in the school,' reveals Ryan. 'I was in the football team and had a toned physique from being overworked at my father's building firm, and I'm ashamed to admit I was really into myself. I had a very big ego – it was all me, me, me.

'So, despite having this lovely girlfriend, I was a complete arse to her, cheating on her with her friends and anyone else I could get my hands on. She was completely blind to this and didn't want to believe it – nor did she want to smash that perfect first love dream.

'Her denial reached the point that even when one night

she caught me in a car getting steamy with one of her friends – her friend's shirt half undone, my top off – she chose to believe my excuse that we were looking for a tape. How can girls be so stupid?

'Anyway, this went on for a couple of years, and then I went to university. She did her final term at school, and then the following year she went to a different university, about a five-hour drive from mine. We continued seeing each other – we were actually very much in love – but I continued being an arse and cheating, cheating, cheating. Finally, I think she grew up and saw that I was a prick. She acknowledged what I was doing and she left me for another guy.

'We don't talk and she still tells her friends that I was the worst boyfriend she ever had!'

Why he forced her to leave

So this is probably quite a depressing example. But what can we really say? Immature men are awful and if they're not ready to grow up, you often can't make them.

As Ryan himself says: 'I think the experience eventually helped to turn me into a nice guy and made me realise the errors of having a big ego. It actually taught me a lot of lessons. First, that my actions could cause a great deal of hurt to someone I loved, and secondly, that I could lose her completely. I think in the end it probably hurt me more than it hurt her, because I was the one that was at fault. I vowed never to cheat again, and though I have had only one other long-term girlfriend since then, I have been one hundred per cent faithful.'

Regrets, they've had a few – not that they'd tell you that . . .

I regretted giving her the heave-ho when . . .

'I saw her looking so hot.'

'A few days after we broke up, I realised she was probably the one holding my life together and, without her, I was just a big kid pretending to be an adult.'

'I found myself alone on Valentine's night.'

'I grew up a bit.'

'She gave me a goodbye kiss that was more like a snog and reminded me of all the good bits of our relationship.'

'The next one turned out to be worse.'

So why do men sabotage relationships for, let's face it, some rather ridiculous reasons?

Sadly, there's no way to dress it up, what we often suspect to be true, is true – without biological clocks to think about they can be commitment-shirking cock-weasels.

As one Jack-the-lad says, 'I'm twenty-seven but I still think I'm sixteen and have all the time in the world. So if I think a girl is "locking down" it automatically freaks me out.'

Yup, we've all identified that rabbit-in-the-headlights look when we've made the mistake of mentioning moving in, getting married or even just going to a friend's wedding together. Apparently, the poor sods just can't cope with enforced and emasculating 'commitment chats' or 'full-on behaviour' or any of the below (oh joy).

The silly things that freak us out

'She wanted us to go on holiday with her parents.'

'I had a dream that she was pregnant and I woke up feeling trapped.'

'She started writing joint Christmas cards to my friends. I wouldn't have minded but the first I knew was when my mates started taking the mick. We'd only been together nine months.'

'She sent me too many texts and called all the time. Then she started turning up at the places she knew I was going to be.'

'She said I had eyes like her father – that's too weird.'

Whilst some of this stuff is ludicrous, there are some little pearls in there too. Clearly, if we try to take too much control, then it is off-putting – so the clever thing is to find a way to make them think commitment issues are all their big idea.

While, sometimes, the damage may be beyond repair, men do confide that there are ways we can reclaim the power when they're being flaky or running a little scared. And it could be as simple as mirroring his behaviour, as one helpful chap admits: 'If he's flaking out on you, simply act in the same way: take longer to text back than he does, don't answer his calls straight away, mess with him the same way he's messing with you, and he'll be putty in your hands.'

Another man-in-the-know suggests you should even put on your poker face and go for broke: 'If a guy is being flaky, the chances are it's because he is no longer interested. So make his decision for him and dump him! If he was being flaky and is still interested, he'll up his game to win you back. If he isn't interested, then you got in there first. You might not have a boyfriend but you'll walk away holding the power!'

Ah, so there you go.

If it did end (and he wasn't nice about it), you were clearly far too good for that gutless wonder anyway. And while there's no excuse for a bad break-up technique, it does bring some comfort to know it's more about them than us. Unfortunately, blokes' dating DNA means they are often notoriously bad at doing the right thing.

The worst way I ended it was ...

'In a phone call when I told her, "Don't bother coming round again." I'd found out she was emailing her ex.'

'By making her do it. I normally just act like an idiot and make them dump me.'

'Probably with some good emotional bullying and cruelty. By pressing the button that you know will hurt her feelings or upset her, but in the heat of an argument you go ahead and say it anyway.'

'By sleeping with her best friend.'

'At Reading service station on the M4. Not the best way to kill a six-year relationship. A heated argument led to me saying all manner of irreversible things. Then we had to get in the car and drive sixty miles home in very awkward silence. This is actually a low point in my life and I have never forgiven myself for being such a tool.'

'By telling her I thought I was gay.'

'I'd tried to tell her it was over a few times, but she didn't believe me. So when she came looking for me one night, I answered the door to my room when there was another girl in my bed.'

'By leaving the country. Twice I packed my bags and scarpered over heartache. It worked too.'

Admittedly, they're a brutal bunch, but it's interesting that many of the guys I questioned admitted that once again it's often the fear of being hurt that turns them into idiots. The truth is they need more reassurance than we'll ever know.

As Alex says, 'In my experience, women expect to be taken care of but they're not really into taking care of their guy. They just get sort of bored or impatient. As a man with a problem, you're on your own.'

He has a good point. I certainly know from my own experiences that sometimes in the past I have wrongly made the assumption that it's all about me. I expected my man to shoulder my problems, to reassure me, to compliment me on the way I looked, to take me on nice dates, to do it all – yet I wasn't really giving anything back. I was too busy flicking my hair 'because I'm worth it' and suffering from a kind of Princess Syndrome.

For all the bravado, men need us to be good to them and

for us to shower them in attention too. The problem is they don't tell us that or actively seek it. They just sulk or say nothing at all, and if you don't bother to worm it out of them, then they start to feel neglected.

And sometimes, in a destructive fashion, this insecurity, fuelled by the out-of-control feeling of being head-over-heels, will manifest itself with some extremely mean behaviour, as Ethan admits . . .

'I'd been dating Justine, a work friend, for six months when she finished with me,' he says. 'We remained friends but I never really exorcised the feelings of pain and I hadn't really forgiven her. A few months later, we got back together during a ski trip. We were getting on really well, but I still felt insecure and, if I'm honest, a little bit bitter about the fact she'd dumped me previously.

'This culminated with a big night out when my friends and I ended up very drunk and half-naked in the street. It was then that a passing hen-do caught sight of us and announced that the bride wanted to be photographed with four naked blokes. Unfortunately, it didn't stop there and the bride wanted a kiss, a big one, which I gave her in front of Justine – with my pants down. Funnily enough, she was not amused.

'We had a big fight and I broke it off saying that it was a bad idea that we got back together. That night during a big row she said she loved me. I was as cold as ice and refused to listen to her. In hindsight, I think I was really hurt that she dumped me the first time, and my pride wanted her to see that I was good for her. I wanted her to regret breaking up with me.

'The thing is that I was a jerk that night and we would have made a great couple.'

Since then, Ethan has moved from one doomed relationship to another, while Justine is now engaged to another man. 'We had a connection that could come once in a lifetime, but I threw it away,' he reckons.

So while we might not believe it, boy, do they chew the cud.

While we're on the subject of bad behaviour, we might as well cover the biggie – why men cheat.

The chaps I interviewed revealed there are many reasons why they do it, but usually it's based around a few key things: insecurities, a subconscious feeling that the relationship is not going to last, excitement and – that old cop-out – their genetic make-up.

'The feeling that you might get caught, or that something terrible will come of your actions is not usually high on the "give-a-fuckometer",' one announces. 'Chasing other women is a drug. When you can get a reaction out of talking to and engaging with another woman, it gives you a buzz. It massages a man's ego with a reaffirmation of his prowess. This excitement can at least seem to outweigh the benefits of a stable loving relationship.'

Yes, I can hear you tutting: if men want to play the field then they should just be done with it and be single, not sneak around chasing birds when they have a loving girlfriend at home. It's a no-brainer.

But the reason these men want to have their cake and eat it is because, well, they think they can. They view love and sex as two separate entities and state the mantra, 'What she doesn't know won't hurt her.'

As one dark horse says, 'I had a girlfriend for many years who I constantly cheated on. It wasn't because she did anything wrong, in fact she couldn't have been better in many ways, it's just that the opportunities were there and it made me feel good. I got a kick out of it; it made me feel alive. The girls I slept with were never up to her standard, but feelings of guilt were far outweighed by the subconscious track record I was keeping of how esteemed I felt.'

But like so many men who recklessly play the field, the dark horse got rumbled. And guess what? When his girlfriend did know and it did hurt – she left.

'It actually took me several years to come to terms with what I had done,' he admits. 'I made really bad choices and realised the hard way that real confidence and self-esteem comes from having a lasting relationship with one special person as nothing can replace that bond.'

I cheated on my girlfriend because . . .

'Lust and insecurity – what other reasons could there be?'

'A bad patch during a long relationship, coupled with alcohol and a very proactive approach from another girl.'

> 'I was drunk and horny, and not really thinking about the consequences.'
>
> 'Because I didn't really love her and had a catastrophic fear of being alone.'

Another guy reveals that a misdemeanour with a work pal was also the biggest mistake he made.

'I didn't want to be unfaithful,' he says. 'In fact, I was really loved up, but there was a girl at work who I would share a laugh and a joke with on a daily basis. It was never anything more than platonic, until we all went away on a work trip to this sixteenth-century chateau in the south of France.

'We had the usual activities and dinner, and then that evening we retired to the bar. After some serious heavy drinking, my work pal and I ended up having a drunken snog. We were heading our separate ways to bed when she asked me in for a nightcap. So there I was in the morning, sneaking out of her bedroom with my crumpled suit on and heading down to breakfast as if nothing had happened. I felt decidedly lousy and was already trying to forget about it.

'We got our flight back and I was just getting my luggage together at Stansted when a text arrived from my girlfriend saying she thought she'd surprise me and pick me up. Suddenly, it was all a little too close to home and I found myself sweating profusely. Determined to make a surreptitious exit, I hung back, saying to the others I would see them in the morning, and went off to the toilet.

'I waited for around ten minutes and then carried my bag sheepishly through the 'Nothing to Declare' (except my stupidity) channel. There, to my horror, I saw all of my team assembled at the barrier waiting for their taxi, and right by my girlfriend, chatting animatedly, was my office "pal".

'My guts were churning and I couldn't look either one of them in the eye for more than a few seconds. It was such a terrible moment and was compounded when my girlfriend offered my work pal a lift. To her credit, she declined and my girlfriend and I wandered off to the car park in silence.

'I felt like the biggest shit imaginable. The fact was my girlfriend wasn't stupid, she knew something was up, and a few weeks later I confessed all. Up until then we'd been really happy, but my actions sparked the beginning of the end.'

I am aware that all this probably makes dismal reading – men admitting and regretting their infidelities doesn't change the fact that they did cheat in the first place.

So what hope is there for womankind when all around men are thoughtlessly cheating because they're horny, insecure, drunk or unhappy? Are all these explanations – coupled with the genetic 'I can't help myself, I'm a man' justification – just well-oiled excuses men trot out to disguise an inane weakness of character or plain selfishness?

Of course, there are studies and theories that will always

purport that men are simply programmed to cheat. But many guys admit this is just a weak excuse and that they still have the capacity to override their 'genes' and put their relationship first.

As Matthew says: 'In long-term relationships, everyone has their moments and opportunities to play away, but what separates us from animals is that we are born with an emotional capacity to make judgements, rather than just act on instinct. Yes, we still have the possibility to be unfaithful, but in the long term it's actually more rewarding and fruitful to be monogamous. You realise you are creating something great together – far greater than you would achieve on your own or by playing the field.'

He also points out that it's not always the guy who is responsible for extra-curricular dalliances. 'We can take responsibility and keep it in our pants if we really want to,' he says. 'But you need to do the same. The other woman in the equation is one of you – and she is just as much to blame as the Neolithic man cheating on his unsuspecting girlfriend.'

Another guy adds: 'I never make excuses about the bad things I've done, and when I had drinks the other night with a friend of mine who knew that I had cheated on the girl I was dating, I admitted I was being unfair. My friend came down on me pretty hard about it – and rightly so, of course. I told her that there was no room for excuses, and that I'm fully aware that it stems from a long-incubated weakness and paranoia that I'm trying very hard to defeat.

'We debated whether or not cheating, while knowing that it's wrong, is better or worse than deceiving yourself about it. The funny epilogue is that I ended up sleeping with her that night.'

So let's hope that little vixen isn't mates with your boyfriend!

Well, it's all getting a bit heavy, isn't it?

If you've left the cheat (he deserved it and, as you now know, probably regrets it), it's time to enjoy your sexy single status. Funnily enough, men just don't buy our protests that girls have a tougher time trying to meet someone nice. In their eyes, it's heaps easier for women to pull.

'Men still have to do the majority of the "wooing",' insists Daniel. 'We have to walk the fine line between showing interest and being sleazy and proving ourselves to be financially viable.'

Another man blasts: 'Do you have any idea how much of a woman's world it is? You have your fancy high-earning jobs, threatening DIY skills and frightening independence. In the good old days, we got to be proper men! You made our dinner and shined our shoes: we were the breadwinners and provided a roof over your heads. Nowadays, we're almost redundant. Hell, you don't even need us to have kids – not when there's the turkey baster option (the stuff of nightmares as far as we're concerned), and the ability to freeze your eggs. You know what you want and you go and get it. And it's intimidating. Yet still I overhear you during your girly lunches in Café Rouge yapping on about the perils of being single and that all the best men are taken – blah, blah, blah.'

Another man urges women to be less suspicious of

approaching men: 'In my view, one of the things that prohibits unions between the sexes the most is that women seem to put up such a defence barrier against meeting potential mates. So many times in bars you see huddles of girls all sitting round, their ranks closed to outsiders. Trying to make eye contact or speak to them is something that is nigh on impossible.

'For a fella, it's a very daunting thing to approach a group of girls – and when we do, it almost requires a kamikaze-style confidence. Not only are you opening yourself up to a merciless rebuttal from one or possibly more girls, but you are also leaving yourself exposed to the other men in the vicinity.' He adds that the competitive nature of men ensures that there is little solidarity – instead they take refuge behind their Heinekens and enjoy the spectacle of the other chap's humiliation unfolding before them.

'It's a uniquely British cycle,' he goes on to claim. 'Lots of booze, little talking and the safety net of ridicule at not being the hapless suitor. If only women could fathom that a conversation between a man and a woman is not always a prelude to a caveman-style attack.'

He probably has a point. If everyone could just relax a little, then perhaps we could all converse without fear of complete rejection – how great would that be? Even if the chemistry is not right, then at least there has been a conversation and no harm has been done.

Incidentally, let's quickly discuss threatening female friends on Facebook. No one likes to see 'witty wall sparring' between your chap and a mystery blonde, but should we be worried that he's actually shagging her?

The general consensus is no, we shouldn't. If a guy is going to cheat, doing it on Facebook is not a given. Although one lad admits, 'It depends on how many times you're poking and throwing sheep at each other . . .'

But it seems the majority of friendships on sites like Facebook are superficial – the odd comment from the girl you once sat next to in Maths and nothing more. So, next time you spot your man's page being smothered in funny retorts and kisses from an unknown lady friend, count to ten and try to breathe!

I guess there is often the temptation for us to overthink the dating world, and we could probably learn a lot from the male attitude to single life. And the first thing the male master class throws up is that we should ignore the fairytales that tell you that being in love is the be-all and end-all.

Well, we kind of knew that already, but I'm feeling charitable, so this fella can have his moment . . .

'Women are constantly told that happiness equals being in love, whereas men seek happiness from friends, sport, hobbies, achievements, careers *and* love,' he says. 'Being single brings a great feeling of freedom – you can go for beers with mates, chase girls and you don't get nagged. You also get to embark on off-the-cuff adventures. I always carry my passport and go abroad at the drop of a hat. More girls should live that way.'

Another wise guy asserts: 'We know that keeping your

plans simple and arranging them at the last minute is an alien concept for you – you might think it's disorganised but it is actually far more efficient than constantly filling your diary weeks in advance.'

Oh dear, the ugly truth about our diary obsession. A time-keeping conflict that has divided the sexes for as long as pink sequinned Filofaxes have existed. Alas, it is true that we have a tendency to book things up months in advance – then at the last minute one friend pulls out because she has a cold or period pains, another is tired, and the last has had a barney with her bloke. Then you have to wait three months for the same thing to occur all over again. We spend half our lives rescheduling, a merry-go-round of over-efficiency.

In contrast, blokes call up their mates that day and go and meet them for a beer because they feel like it. No one's disappointed; no one's stood up. Bob's your uncle. Perhaps we could learn something there.

And just a little footnote from Joel: 'When you ask a girl out and she tells you she's busy for the next three weeks, we view it as a brush off, so you're not doing yourself any favours there.' A valid point.

So what next? Well, single life for men, of course, brings the joy of seeing other women naked. But let's not pretend we're prissy; there is something very exciting about getting lustful over a new, hot man.

If you've been stuck with a skinny, but out-of-shape man all these months (moobs and a pigeon chest – possibly the worst combination?), then surely the prospect of now pulling a bronzed Adonis ignites the same spark?

And as for our ridiculous body hang-ups, we need to lose them. As one man says: 'Women concern themselves with fantasy body issues, such as cellulite and wobbly tummies, which don't even register with us. In fact, a woman who is comfortable and confident with her body gives off a very sexy signal that drives us wild.'

When men think of the additional bonuses to single life, apparently there are plenty. Not having to answer to anyone but themselves, choosing their own leisure activities, never having to go shopping or visit our family (*grr*) and watching whatever they want, whether it's football or porn or (very secretly) *Love Actually*. Again, all things we lovely ladies can capitalise on.

What attracts chaps most is when we radiate a sense of fun that helps keep the relationship fresh.

'We want you to be the girl we first met,' says Declan. 'The girl who loved adventures, going out and having a wicked time with us. Also, and this might seem strange, we like you to keep us on our toes. By reminding us that you are attractive, interested in other pursuits and confident, you will keep us entranced. You can afford to keep a bit of mystery back as it's when we have everything on a plate that we get complacent. By doing this, by being gregarious and interested in our friends and family, you'll find you make us happy.'

He adds that when girlfriends decide suddenly that they don't want to go out, get angry because their chaps have gone on a random bender, or throw their toys out of prams for trivial reasons, it really does grate.

'Please – and this is very important,' he insists, 'try, try, try not to fall into the trap of being a nutter. This affects nine out of ten women. For whatever reason, for whatever atrophy of hormones, remember: think it but don't say it! Being a nutter will result in a man's wilted self-esteem, rapid emasculation and fading empathy.

'There is nothing worse for a bloke than having to contend with the whims of a female mind going off on its own tangent because of what we've supposedly done or because we don't operate in the same psychological stratosphere as you do. It's very important – if you are going to do or say something that we find trivial, nagging or random – to add in the precursor "I know this might seem/sound a bit mental . . ." At least then we can forgive you for what you do, or celebrate it, even, in a kooky kind of way.

'Otherwise, and this is the best part, we do essentially want to try and impress you; it's our *raison d'être*. Sometimes it's just difficult to show it. All of our various relationship conundrums are because we are trying our damnest to make sure we can get the prize at the end of the day. You are the ones holding us together, keeping our feet on the ground and giving us the will to carry on! So don't go changing.'

Yay!

The truth about men (by men)

'We don't always pee standing up. There. I said it.'

'We're more like you than you think. We just control our emotions while a lot of women are controlled by theirs.'

'If you just let things take their natural course, it will either work or it won't. For God's sake stop basing the state of your relationships on a group decision from your mates or on examples set by Manolo Blahnik-wearing street walkers on *Sex and the City*!'

'We are all little boys in adult bodies.'

'If we're acting weird, then there's definitely something up. Ask, ask and ask again; you'll eventually get the truth out of us!'

'We are simple beasts. But don't be fooled by other people's perceptions, deep down we're sensitive souls too.'

'We actually want the same things from women as they do from us. It's just that we all want different things at different times. I believe the key is bumping into the right girl at the right time when you both want the same thing. It's a lottery but we need to be in it to win it.'

'We're all individuals, there is no one universal truth. Oh, hang on, yes there is. We all like tits.'

Conclusion
A Freemale State of Mind

Well, I sincerely hope you've enjoyed gasping at other people's sorry sagas and calamitous chronicles. Hopefully, it has been an opportunity to see that everyone has form – whether it was the time you went a bit crazy after a boyfriend ditched you, the wicked revenge you extracted on a cheating ex, or the realisation you did actually cause hurt.

Over the years, we've all been trampled on or broken someone's heart or stolen (whether on purpose or not) another girl's boyfriend. We've mistaken lust for love, committed a betrayal, two-timed or wised up. But, just like DNA, all your ups and downs have intertwined to create your own unique and invaluable blueprint. It makes you the person you are and guides you on your way. It also gives your friends *lots* to laugh about.

If you've just read this book for nostalgia or for the sport of laughing at other people's bonkers behaviour (it's allowed), then I'm pretty much done with you. I hope you enjoyed it. But if you're still smarting after a break-up, read on.

If nothing else, I hope the real-life trials and tribulations told candidly in this book will indicate that you are not alone. As you walk along the street, you'd be surprised what torturous thoughts people are hiding inside as they bravely face up to the challenges of failed romances. It's a tough world out there. But what happens when the going gets tough? That's right – the tough get going (right now I hope you are hearing the sounds of Billy Ocean and jumping up and down faux boxing in a Mr Motivator stylee).

So what have you learned at Broken Heart Boot Camp? Hopefully, you've seen that you are stronger and more resilient than you ever thought possible. Perhaps you've realised that there's always someone worse off than you. You now have clarity to see that you can't stay in and mope all the time. Instead, you will wash your hair, put on your make-up, make yourself look great, hold your head up and go out with your friends when they invite you. You'll do your crying later, at least after you've attempted to have a bit of fun.

You now know that being single creates amazing opportunities. You can do all those things that you put on hold, and fulfil all those ambitions and dreams that fell by the wayside while you were tied down.

If you're still smarting, then you've got all the proof that you will get over the pain in time – and you will be a better person for it. All the worry, sleepless nights, panic attacks and depression are eventually going to fade because you will work to make them fade.

As for the procrastinators out there – in an ideal world we would be grown-up and mature enough to know when to end a relationship, but sometimes we're a little bit cowardly and even if we've realised we're not in love any more, we just can't take that final step to end a romance.

It might be because we don't want to go to that wedding on our own, or because it's nearly Christmas or our birthday or his mum is just so lovely and she'd be heartbroken if we split up.

Or it could be that you just don't want to be the only single girl among your friends who all seem so happily coupled up. But trust me, dumping someone three days after they've bought you a gorgeous (and very expensive) present will only make you feel worse or give you the excuse to put the break-up off for yet another few weeks or months.

Most of the time this kind of thing doesn't cross men's minds. They decide they want to split up and they just do it. Sometimes they're brave enough to say the words, other times they just behave so badly you have to finish things for them.

If he's not being nice, then sticking around in the hope that one day he'll realise you are actually his soulmate is going to hurt just one person – YOU. Of course, nobody wants to break up; it's like admitting you're a failure. No matter what you did, you just couldn't make the relationship work. But most of the time, you are splitting up for a very good reason and you'll feel much better afterwards.

There's no point clinging on to a dying relationship – you'll always be able to find excuses to stick around – but if there's something missing or your love is damaged beyond all repair, it's going to stay like that until you get out. Chances are, if you're not happy, he won't be either, and it's time one of you found the guts to take the plunge and end things while you've still got the chance of a civil conversation. It's time to wake up and smell the coffee. Do the deed – or accept that he's done it to you.

The fact is, if a relationship is going to work, you both need to feel the same way and really want it to. It doesn't matter how much you're in love with him, would die for him, want his kids, dream of walking down the aisle to be welcomed by his smiling face – if his vision is not the same as yours, it won't happen.

So no matter whether he broke it off or you did, you have to see it as a fresh start. Take a deep breath and put your best foot forward – you are as ready as you will ever be to embrace single life. Perhaps you won't feel quite like leaping off into the sunset shouting, 'Bugger blokes!', but you are on your way to better times. As Alana will testify . . .

'When I split up with my ex-fiancé, I thought it was the end of the world,' she says. 'I wrote in my diary that there was a big black hole where my life was supposed to be. What the hell was I supposed to do now?

'It took me time to realise, but when I was with him, I was stressed, miserable, poor and even in debt. A friend has since told me that I didn't smile much. I am now, in no particular order, more successful, debt-free, earning more, thinner, happier and healthier. I am going out with a fantastic guy who is much nicer and better looking than my ex. So I'm very glad we broke up.'

When the chips are down, you can turn a corner and do things you never dreamt possible – but allowing your friends to help you on your way is vital.

When Lily became pregnant at the age of twenty, her

previously adoring boyfriend dutifully hung around – but rather reluctantly. He was suddenly quite busy and Lily was forced to consider what to do by herself. As she was debating her options, it was decided for her when she suffered a miscarriage. Afterwards, Lily was in despair. She and her boyfriend tried to keep it together but her depression, mood swings and resentment made her hard to be around. He was young and meant to be having the time of his life, and so eventually he left her.

Thankfully, this is where her best friend swooped into action. 'Jane was my lifeline,' she reveals. 'I looked terrible, so first she did my highlights, then she came round with wine, chocolate and fruit, and we watched *Sex and the City* DVDs. Then she persuaded me to go for long walks on the beach. It made me realise that I wanted to get away. Although Jane offered to come with me, I decided to go off abroad on my own.'

So for two months Lily went to work in a ski resort for the holiday season. 'I knew the only way I'd feel OK again was to scare the shit out of myself and survive,' she now says.

And that is what it's all about. Facing your fear of the unknown and taking the plunge anyway. If you're used to having a man around, to being the other half of a pair, it's bound to feel different being on your own, particularly after a long relationship. But now is the perfect time to go for a goal or a challenge. You have the opportunity to find that new job, go travelling or better yourself by learning something you find interesting.

You can build your confidence and go back into the

dating world – if you want to. Or you can be satisfyingly selfish and spoil yourself. So change your flat around, eat crisps in bed at midnight, watch a weepy film until the early hours of the morning without withering comments from your ex. You can do EXACTLY what you want to do.

Or, if being selfish just isn't your thing, there are loads of good causes out there that need sensitive, kind people like you to help them with their workload. It will make you feel wanted again, just when you need it most. If you're feeling wobbly, chances are that soon you will be more resilient, self-sufficient and able to cope with just about anything – just as you were before.

And just in case you feel like the only single freak in town, you couldn't be more wrong. The number of single women out there has more than doubled in the last thirty years. Hordes of bright, clever, brilliant women are refusing to settle for rubbish relationships and are embracing single life instead.

We all have moments when we get the fear about meeting The One or allow ourselves to be teased about ticking biological clocks, but it's about doing what's right for you. Maybe you felt undervalued in your relationship, maybe he belittled you and you'd lost the sense of who you are. Maybe he cheated; maybe you just drifted apart. But if deep down that niggling feeling tells you it's fundamentally not right and you can be brave enough to seek something better, then daring to go it alone will gives you a vital chance to reclaim your independence and rediscover the real you.

That doesn't mean you have to claim you never want to

meet a man, or get married or have babies – far from it. It's just about building up your self-esteem and confidence, and not compromising on your hopes or dreams (all things we now know men find attractive too). Once you've set all that in place, you'll be ready for anything.

So gear yourself up for the heady rush when you first clap eyes on him and experience that intoxicating chemistry all over again . . .

Acknowledgements

There are so many people I need to thank and I will start with Carly Cook, my brilliant, funny and workaholic editor. You are an absolute star.

I'd like to thank everyone at Headline, especially Josh Ireland, Emily Furniss, Jo Liddiard, Helena Towers, Ant Gatt and Ruth Jeffery for their hard work and continued support. Thanks you also to my literary agent Amanda Preston.

This book would never have come together without all the amazing insight and recollections of those who shared their stories. Thank you so much for your brilliant contributions and I hope you enjoy seeing your secrets immortalised in print.

I must give particular thanks to Rachael Wright, Scarlett Russell, Laura Johnson, Laura Topham, Isabel Mohan, Heidi Stephens and Sarah Finley for the enthusiasm, encouragement and insight. I've been a complete book bore and you have been very patient.

Thank you to Mark Frith and Flic Everett for your guidance and expertise and also to Stefan Maingot at Blue Cake for the digital genius.

I also owe big thanks to all the Golden Goose gang – Miki Watson, Laura Wood, Laura Hind, Felicity Hardingham,

Remy Le Ferve and Katie Hancock – for all the brilliant ideas and suggestions.

Last, but by no means least, thank you to my mum Judy, my wonderful friend Clare Fitzsimons and my beau Joseph for all the love, help and support you have continually given me. You are the best.

If you've enjoyed this book, then please visit my website: www.charlotteward.net

More Non-fiction from Headline

WHY AM I ALWAYS THE ONE BEFORE 'THE ONE'?

CHARLOTTE WARD

Charlotte Ward had always believed that after a
few serious boyfriends, some unsuitable encounters,
and the odd broken heart, she would find the right guy
and all would be happy ever after.

However, towards the end of her 20s, it had become
clear that finding Mr Right was actually pretty tricky.
In fact, she'd soon realised that every boyfriend she'd
whipped into shape and then broken up with had settled
down with someone else almost immediately. The training
that Charlotte had given them had set them up for life
– just not life with her.

In this witty, intimate memoir, Charlotte shares her
experiences and insights on dating, breaking up and
starting over again. It wasn't an easy journey, but now
happily settled with 'The Beau', has Charlotte finally
reached the coveted status of 'The One' . . . ?

NON-FICTION / RELATIONSHIPS 978 0 7553 1815 5